**NORSE ARMADA** An invasion of England by the Danes is represented in a 12th-century English illuminated manuscript showing scenes from the life of St Edmund, the 9th-century king of East Anglia.

**Arctic Circle**

Iceland

Viking route
Area of Danelaw
X Site of battle

0          300 km
0      200 miles

ATLANTIC
OCEAN

NORWEGIAN
SEA

Iceland and Greenland

**Faroe
Islands**

Shetland
Islands

**Orkney
Islands**

Trondheim

NORWEGIANS

Gulf of Bothnia

Urnes
Borgund
Bergen

Oseberg
Gokstad

SWEDES

Uppsala
Birka
Helgö

Russian

Russian rivers

Paviken
**Gotland**
Öland

BALTIC
SEA

NORTH
SEA

Lindholm Høje
Fyrkat
**Jutland**

Jelling
Vorbasse
Ravning Enge
Ribe

Skuldelev
Sjaelland
**DANES**
Trelleborg

Army
Road

Hedeby

Iona

Lindisfarne

Jarrow    Wearmouth
NORTHUMBRIA
Isle of Man

Kintyre

Rathlin
Island

Tara
980 X
Dublin X Clontarf
1014
**Ireland**

Limerick

Waterford
Cork

Wicklow

York X Stamford Bridge
1066
**Britain**

Nottingham   Lincoln
Derby
Repton  Trent
Stamford
MERCIA  EAST
ANGLIA

Edington
878 X          Thames
WESSEX

Hamburg
Elbe

Frisia

Dorestad

Scheldt   Antwerp

Rhine

Vistula

Amiens
Rouen
Beauvais
Bayeux
Evreux   Meaux
Seine  Paris
Melun
Chartres

Angers   Orléans

Nantes
Loire  Tours
Noirmoutier

**FRANKISH
EMPIRE**

Bay of Biscay

Limoges
Angoulême
Périgueux
Bordeaux
Garonne
Toulouse

Aquitaine

Spain and Mediterranean Sea

**The Vikings in
the wider world**

Helluland   Greenland

Markland

Reykjavik   Area shown on main map
**Iceland**

Vinland

ATLANTIC
OCEAN

Staraya Ladoga
Novgorod

**KIEVAN**   Smolensk
**RUSSIA**   Volga
Dnieper
Kiev

BLACK SEA
Mikligard
(Constantinople)

Lisbon
Seville
Cadiz   MEDITERRANEAN SEA

Baghdad

Strait of
Gibraltar

Rhône
Pisa
Danube

nowadays. Denmark was larger, taking in parts of modern Sweden and also extending farther south. Norway also included parts of modern Sweden. At the beginning of the Viking Age, Denmark was more or less united under one king, while in Norway local kings and chieftains each ruled over distinct districts. Sweden was ruled by an ancient line of kings. In all three countries, the kings were elected by the local *things*, or assemblies of free men, although they usually came from the established royal families. A common language was spoken throughout Scandinavia, from which individual languages subsequently developed in each country.

### 'THEY RAVAGE, THEY DESTROY'

The Viking Age lasted from the 8th to the 11th centuries, beginning in the 790s with a hurricane of raids on foreign shores. Various reasons have been suggested for the sudden breakout from Scandinavia. One was a shortage of good farmland. In Norse tradition, when a farmer died his eldest son took over the land, and younger sons had to go elsewhere to make a living. Additionally, dynastic wars in Norway – for example, when Harald Finehair imposed his rule over the whole of Norway in the 880s, and when Eirik I was ousted in 934 – caused warrior chiefs to flee with their armed men, and the development of seagoing longships in the 750s opened up new opportunities to threaten foreign lands.

The nature of the breakout was not the same throughout Scandinavia, however. Swedish Vikings were primarily traders, and followed the rivers Dnieper and Volga south and east through Russia to the Black Sea and the Caspian Sea. It was the Vikings of Denmark and Norway who headed west towards the wealthy, ill-defended coasts of Britain and northern France. Here, it appears, the temptation to loot rather than trade was overpowering.

The attacks are well documented by horrified clerics who had no clear idea who the seaborne warriors were or where they came from. The raiders were variously described as 'pagans', 'northmen', 'strangers' or 'shipmen'. The term 'Viking' was just one of these expressions and its origins are unclear. The Norse word *vik* means bay, creek or fiord, and some scholars have suggested that to go *i viking* originally meant to quit one's inlet and go adventuring abroad.

UNCOVERING THE PAST Excavations at Coppergate in York have revealed evidence of a bustling Viking trade centre that flourished in northern England.

The victims of their aggression have provided vivid accounts of the Vikings' exploits. A French monk, describing the Danes' siege of Paris in 885, refers to the raiders as 'wild beasts going by horse and foot through hill and field . . . killing babies, children, young men, old men, fathers, sons, and mothers . . . They ravage, they destroy, they burn.' The onslaughts on France and Germany are narrated in the *Frankish Annals*, and the struggle against the Vikings during 893-7 is an important theme of the *Anglo-Saxon Chronicle*, a year-by-year narrative of the history of England.

Such accounts, however, have perhaps distorted the picture of Norse life that posterity has inherited, and other sources of information do exist. For example, a Muslim writer, Ibn Fadlan, met and left a lengthy description of Viking traders in Russia, perceiving them as

GLASS BEADS Viking jewellery and trinkets, like these from Sweden, reveal a love of colour and ornament.

LONGHOUSE   A Norse building has been reconstructed at the Trelleborg settlement in Denmark.

uncouth, but not as a blind force of destruction. And *The Deeds of the Archbishop of Hamburg*, written by Adam of Bremen in about 1075, provides a picture of Norsemen living in their homeland towards the close of the Viking Age. Adam distinguished clearly between the three Scandinavian countries. Norway, he wrote, was an especially inhospitable land inhabited by sturdy and frugal herdsmen whose harsh lives turned them into brave fighters. The soil of Jutland (Denmark's northern peninsula) was barren too: 'Apart from areas of land near the rivers, the region appears a waste and desert land.'

Adam seems only to have visited Denmark, and reported on Norway and Sweden at second hand. Much of what he writes is simplified or misleading: Jutland was covered with inhospitable heath, but was by no means bereft of human population – recent research indicates that the area was scattered with villages. Nevertheless, his testimony presents a more complex picture of Viking life than that bequeathed by the monks in Europe's monasteries.

### RUNES AND SAGAS

The Scandinavians of this time wrote no histories of their own, but memories of past events did survive in the Norse sagas – heroic narratives written down in Iceland from about 1200. They were based on tales told around the fireside, learnt by heart and handed down from generation to generation.

Stories range from tales of the pagan gods to family narratives and fictionalised chronicles of Norwegian kings. Though riddled with fantasy and exaggeration – and committed to writing long after the events they purported to describe – the sagas nonetheless incorporate much fascinating historical material. Poems, riddles and proverbs have also survived, along with rune stones – memorial stones carved with inscriptions in runes, the Norsemen's alphabetical writing system.

Clues to life in Viking times come also from archaeological finds; these range from Norse city sites and the hulks of entire longships to gold coins, bone flutes, iron locks and ivory chessmen. Cold and waterlogged soils in Scandinavia helped to preserve everyday items of leather and wood that would have perished in milder environments; shoes and boots exist, with their careful stitching intact. Modern technology has enhanced the picture. Microscopes with ×400 magnification have permitted scientists to identify pollen grains at sites, so determining what plants were known to the Vikings. Modern medical analysis of bodies found in Norse graves has revealed the diseases that afflicted people. In 1990 it proved possible, through laser and computer technology, to reconstruct the face of a Viking from a skull found in York.

PROTECTION MONEY   Coins like these were extorted from the English by the Vikings.

# LIFE ON THE FARMSTEAD

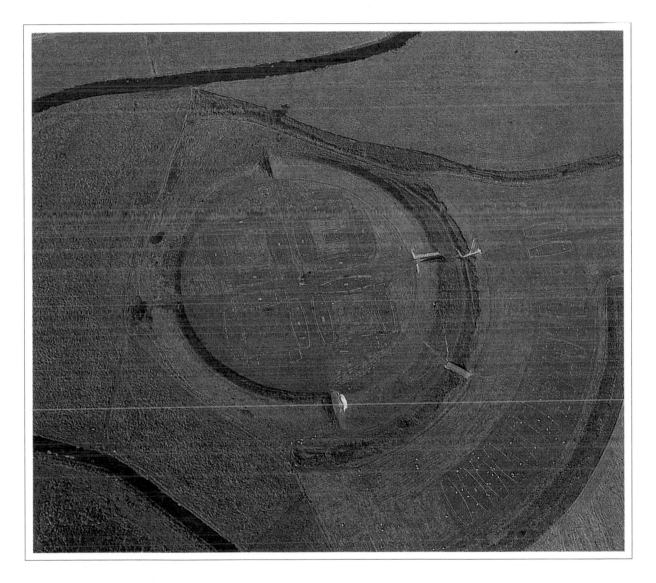

An aerial view shows the grass-covered ramparts of Trelleborg fortress
on the island of Sjaelland in Denmark. Viking lands are still imprinted with traces
of the hardy farmer-warriors who once built strongholds and homesteads there.
Trelleborg was not a war fort but an administrative centre where taxes
were collected. In the farmlands around, families worked fields and tended flocks
much like other European peoples of the time.

# INSIDE THE VIKING HOME

Stern mountains, sullen marshes, dank forests and glowing lava fields – all were familiar

to the Viking homesteader. Scandinavian families would put down roots at the very wilderness edge

as long as they could find a few pockets of fertile soil.

T HE VIKINGS were basically a farming people whose home life was rooted in the *baer*, or farmstead, with its cluster of homes, stables, barns, boathouses and smithy. A wood-lined well was a common feature of many settlements, and trackways of tightly packed logs sometimes ran between the buildings, offering some protection against the mud that clogged the most heavily used paths. With the damp northern climate, sodden ground must have been the bane of everyday life. The wooden walls of Viking buildings often rested on a row of stones laid down to prevent timbers

from rotting. On this stone sill, too, the builders sometimes laid down flooring planks for insulation and protection against decay.

In many cases, the outline of the sill stones provides the only evidence of a rural settlement in Scandinavia; though traces of post-holes have survived, nothing above ground level remains of the

**NORWEGIAN LANDSCAPE  The Viking homeland was mazed with fiords, lakes, rivers and streams. For communication, farmers as well as fishermen had to become skilled boatmen.**

farmhouses themselves. However, clues to their appearance come from town buildings, which have survived much better, and from the urban examples it is clear that the Vikings were familiar with several different methods of building in wood. These included 'log-cabin' construction, making walls of horizontal logs jointed at the ends. Another method was to attach vertical or horizontal planking to corner posts. Houses were designed to a fairly common plan. The length of a log building was determined by the length of the tree trunks available in the forests. As a result, dwellings were sometimes built up in blocks of independent units joined together. Where timber was scarce the Vikings also filled in walls with wattle and daub, using woven panels of slender branches or reeds, plastered with mud or clay.

Most farm buildings were likely to have been relatively plain and functional in appearance. However, excavations have shown that early churches from the Viking period were adorned with splendid

FORBIDDING LAND  Moss and lichens cover a lava field in Iceland, settled by Norsemen in about 870.

carved and painted decorations, and it is a fair guess that a wealthy farmer-warrior might also have had the exterior of his home embellished, if not in so grand a manner.

The shape of the typical farm dwelling was an

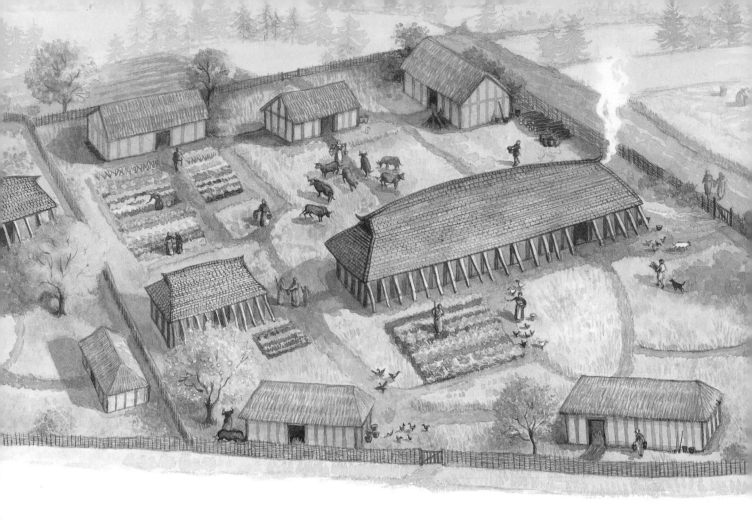

FARMING VILLAGE   Denmark's level terrain was better suited to agriculture than were the mountainous regions of Norway and Sweden, and sizable farming communities grew up there. This is part of Vorbasse in central Jutland, where seven farms clustered together within a compound. Individual farms were fenced off from their neighbours. Around each main dwelling were smithy, barns and huts that may have housed slave-labourers.

oblong, from which the term 'longhouse' derives. Either rectangular, or with curved walls, it was roofed with thatched straw or reeds. Where timber was very scarce, the Vikings used turf as an all-purpose building material. Sometimes the farmers roofed sod houses with turf and let the grass in it keep on growing, to help to keep the house warm. It is easy to picture such farmsteads emerging almost organically from the landscape, as the peat huts of Ireland's peasantry did until very recent times. Such dwellings cannot have been particularly comfortable, but the main thing for the Viking was to have a roof over his head.

### SMOKE AND SOOT

Inside the longhouse was a single room where the whole family ate, slept, worked and entertained their friends. It was snug, dark, smelly and smoky, with soot-blackened rafters and a huge fireplace,

edged with stones, at the centre. Chimneys were unknown – fumes escaping through a hole in the roof, or through gaps in the roof and gables. Family members sat and slept on simple benches or on fur-covered earth platforms around the walls, the most important members of the household closest to the fire. Servants and slaves were relegated to the colder recesses, and may even have shared stabling with the animals in the byre sited close to the

### HOT BATHS

Icelandic Vikings took advantage of the country's volcanic hot springs in order to take a bath. They performed their ablutions in open-air pools of natural hot water, which they also used to wash their laundry. One Norseman's farm there was called *Laugar* – literally, Baths.

longhouse. This served for crop storage and often contained cattle stalls, too. The animals must have been noisy and smelly companions, but they provided a useful source of heat.

Viking families were more concerned that their homes should be warm than that they should be airy or well lit, and many of their dwellings were entirely windowless. Sometimes, at the gable end, there was a small aperture covered with a stretched pig's bladder or with the membrane of a newborn calf to let in a hint of light (glass panes were unknown). For lighting they used oil lamps or more costly wax candles, which increased the fug in the longhouse. Historians speculate that many Vikings suffered from chronic carbon-dioxide poisoning, at its worst in winter when more time was spent indoors. And if the Vikings are characterised as clannish and quarrelsome, beset by blood ties and blood feuds, the fact must owe much to the huddled congestion of longhouse life. It is possible to imagine sheer human claustrophobia as a spur to go adventuring abroad – an important motive for the whole phenomenon of Viking expansion.

Furniture was scanty. It is known, both from grave finds and from Norse literature, that wealthy Vikings slept on handsome carved beds with mattresses stuffed with feathers and down, but these can only have been for the most privileged members of society. In the average rural longhouse, the main items were the benches and earth platforms around the walls. Low stools were also fairly common in Viking homes, but chairs were rarer and there were no cup-

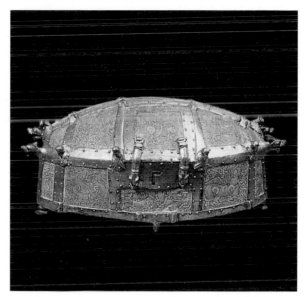

HOUSEHOLD CONTAINER  Family treasures were kept in lockable boxes; this one is shaped like a house.

boards. Coins, jewellery, fine fabrics and other valuables were stored in wooden chests, secured with a twist key of the modern type or with a 'barrel padlock', a cylinder lock held shut by splayed metal prongs. To force the prongs together and open the lock, the user inserted a special key with a perforated plate at the end. Examples of this type of mechanism have been recovered from the Viking dig at Coppergate in York.

The wealthy farmer, no less than the prosperous merchant, might well have a store of riches locked away in some part of his dwelling. *Egil's Saga* describes an occasion on which the hero and his men are held prisoner by a rich and powerful farmer. They manage to free themselves from their bonds and go looking for loot: 'Aki went to where there was a trapdoor in the wooden floor and opened it, saying

ICELANDIC TURF HOUSES  Where building timber was scarce, the Vikings improvised with whatever materials were to hand.

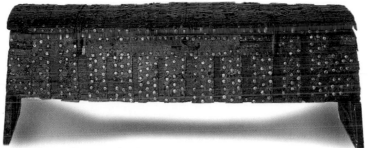

**VIKING BENCH** Chairs were rare items in the Viking longhouse; benches were better suited to communal life.

that they should go down into the room below. They took lights with them and went down. There was the farmer's strong-room, fine trea-sures and much silver. The men loaded themselves and came out. Egil took for himself a good, big treasure-chest and carried it under his arm. Then they went to the wood.' It says much about Viking psychology that the episode left Egil feeling that they had acted dishonourably – like common thieves rather than as warriors taking revenge. So, according to the saga, he went back to the farm, took a log from the fire and thrust the blazing end under the eaves of the building. As the roof caught fire and the farm's occupants tried to flee, Egil stood at the door and felled anyone who attempted to get out. Honour satisfied, he then returned to the wood and rejoined his companions.

Apart from the lockable chest, the Vikings' main storage device was the hook on the wall: buckets, pots, sacks, tools and weapons cluttered all parts of the longhouse. Straw and hay covered the stamped earth or planking floor, and archaeologi-cal evidence indicates that the ground was littered with food scraps and bits of household rubbish.

Conditions must have been very unhygienic: slops were dumped just outside the house and the Viking toi-let was often little more than a hole in the ground out-side, with clumps of moss used for lavatory paper. But the Norsemen were not wholly careless of personal cleanliness. An Icelandic saga speaks of a guest being met at table by his host 'with a greeting and a towel', and from other sources it appears that Saturday was specially noted

**COLLAPSIBLE BED** This article, from the Oseberg ship, was easily dismantled, perhaps for travel.

# THE SCANDINAVIAN CHARACTER

THE GERMAN MONK Adam of Bremen, writing in about 1075, described the Viking approach to life: ❛ All Nordic people are noted for their hospitality, but the Swedes excel. They consider it shameful to deny good cheer to a traveller, and they compete keenly with one another for the privilege of entertaining him. The stranger is welcome among them for as long as he likes, and they take it in turns to look after his wellbeing during his stay … Norway is the most remote land in the world. Because of its wild mountains and extreme cold, it is the least productive of countries, suitable only for herds. The people browse their cattle far off in the lonely places, and so manage to live off their livestock, using milk for food and skins for clothing. Their country breeds many bold warriors who attack more often than they face attack, for they have not been softened by rich harvests. ❜

**DAILY CHORES** The axe was an essential, all-purpose tool, as necessary for chopping firewood and timber for building as it was for war.

# FISHING AND WHALING

BUTCHERING A WHALE  The great sea mammal supplied the Vikings with lamp oil and skins as well as food.

SCANDINAVIA has an extraordinarily long coastline relative to its land area. With a multitude of offshore islands and innumerable fiords, rivers and streams, it is small wonder that the people became accomplished boatmen. They became keen fishermen, too. While lakes and rivers provided the likes of pike and salmon, the Baltic Sea and North Atlantic and Arctic oceans offered rich harvests of cod, haddock and herring to enterprising navigators. Despite the cold climate, even the northernmost harbours were kept ice-free through the winter by the warm flow of the Gulf Stream. In northern Norway especially, the Vikings relied heavily on fishing and whaling as a means of livelihood.

Household rubbish tips excavated at Viking sites have yielded thousands of fishbones, as well as the remains of countless eels and oyster shells. Archaeologists have also discovered fishing equipment which proves that the Vikings used barbed iron hooks, nets and harpoons. Seals and walruses were speared where they were found, while whales were driven ashore for the kill. A Norwegian chieftain named Ottar visited the court of England's King Alfred, who wrote in about 890 that the Viking's country offered the best whale-hunting in the world: 'Along with five other crews he killed sixty of them in two days.' A whale furnished the hunters with fat, oil and skins for clothing as well as providing nourishment, but it seems that even among the Vikings it was not an entirely familiar food. A story in *Eirik's Saga* records how a party of hungry Greenlanders once came upon a stranded whale and rushed to cut it up. 'No one recognised what kind of whale it was, not even Karlesfini, who was an expert on whales. The cooks boiled the meat, but when it was eaten it made them all ill.'

FISHERMAN'S FRIEND  A 'leister' was used to spear salmon and other fish.

# THE VIKING VILLAGE

VIKING VILLAGES often grew up at the water's edge, and on low-lying meadowland streets were covered with wooden planking to prevent them from becoming muddy. In the foreground of the settlement depicted here, a village craftsman is forging arrow tips, using bellows to heat the forge fire. All around, the community bustles with activity as inhabitants tend their livestock, tan skins, dry fish and bring in timbers for repairs and new building work. Thatched with straw and reeds, the longhouses are walled with logs or planks arranged both vertically and horizontally. Some dwellings are buttressed by sloping timbers placed at regular intervals outside to support the top of the walls against the weight of the roof. Many of the homes have their own fenced-in plot where work is done and animals are penned. There is no evidence, however, that the Scandinavians practised gardening.

# THE VIKING YEAR

Apart from the seasonal rituals of ploughing, sowing and harvesting – and the multitude

of day-to-day chores in boathouse, barn and smithy – Norse farmers also enlivened their

annual calendar with profitable raiding excursions overseas.

FAVOURITE ANIMAL   The Vikings loved horses, which are depicted here on a tapestry from the Oseberg ship.

THE VIKING FARM was self-sufficient. Not only did people grow their own food and brew their own beer, they also made their own clothes, blankets and sailcloth, weaving them on an upright loom propped against the wall of every longhouse. The loom had a horizontal beam from which the warps or vertical threads hung down, weighted by stones or baked clay rings resembling ring-doughnuts. Spinning and weaving were considered to be women's work, and must have

occupied much of their time, day in, day out.

Though linen and hempen cloth were both used by the Vikings, the flax from which they are made was grown only in southern Scandinavia, and the most common fabric was wool. Women sheared the sheep, combed out the wool to get rid of any tangles, and then spun the yarn. Many fragments of textiles have survived, and they show that Viking women employed a wide range of weaving

RICH TRAPPINGS   Wooden harness-bows
were often beautifully carved.

**STRIP FARMING  Farmers used a wooden harrow to loosen the earth before sowing seeds. Left: A field at Lindholm Hoje, Denmark, is still marked by Viking farmers' furrows.**

techniques to create different patterned effects in the cloth. Today the relics appear dull in hue, but laboratory analysis has revealed that they were once brightly coloured by dyes made from plants such as madder for red, woad for blue and weld for yellow. It is thought that the mordant needed to fix the dyes to the textiles was obtained from club moss.

### WITH SWORD AND SEED BASKET

Spinning and weaving were year-round activities, but many other jobs were done according to the seasonal patterns imposed by long and bitter winters. Spring was the time for ploughing and sowing

the arable fields around the farmstead. Fertile soil was scarce in Scandinavia, and in mountainous Norway, especially, it was confined to a few areas – chiefly the strips of land around the fiords or narrow inlets that run deep inland from the sea. Much of Sweden was covered by marsh, lake and forest. The biggest tracts of arable land were found in Denmark, though even this more promising terrain was strewn with sandy heathland and bog. Equipment was, moreover, fairly primitive. Throughout most of the Viking period, farmers used a crude plough known as an ard to break up the ground. Made of wood, it amounted to little more than a crooked stick with a point, and it only scraped a furrow in the earth, without turning it over. While the ploughman guided the device, the ard was dragged along by an ox or by a human assistant. A heavier plough, with an iron-shod share, wheel and mouldboard, arrived only very late in the Viking period.

The imprint of furrows made by Viking farmers was revealed in the 1950s at Lindholm Hoje, Denmark, when a huge sand drift was cleared away. The wind-blown sand seems to have covered the field during a storm in the 11th century, for its removal revealed the ground just as it had been then, complete with footprints and wheeltracks. The broad beds were corrugated with neatly spaced furrows

---

**EYEWITNESS**

# IN PRAISE OF A FAVOURITE OX

VIKING FARMERS valued their animals, as the *Laxdaela Saga* shows: ❛ Olaf the Peacock had many valuable beasts among his livestock. He had a magnificent ox called Harri, dapple grey in colour, and bigger than any other cattle. He had four horns: two of them were large and well placed, the third stood straight up in the air, and the fourth grew out of his forehead and curled down below his eyes; he used this horn for breaking ice. He used to scrape the snow with his hooves, like a horse, to get at the grass. ❜

# FREY AND FREYA – GOD AND GODDESS OF THE FARM

VIKING FARMERS believed that if the crops were to flourish and grow tall, sacrifices must be made to the fertility god, Frey, who was said to bestow peace and pleasure on mortals.

Frey represented the marriage of sky and earth that produced the spring. At sowing time his statue was carried from village to village in a blossom-decked cart and welcomed with flowers and sacrifices of boars, the animal sacred to Frey.

**FERTILITY GOD   A bronze statuette of the lusty Frey, from Sweden.**

Frey's name crops up in place names throughout Scandinavia: a particularly fruitful field might be called *Freysakr* (Frey's cornfield), too, as the means by which fertility was introduced .

Frey had a female partner in the shape of his sister, Freya – their names mean 'master' and 'mistress' respectively. Goddess of love and fruitfulness, Freya went about in a carriage drawn by cats, searching for her lost husband, Od, and weeping tears that turned to gold. She was invoked by childless women in the hope of giving birth. So widespread was her worship that one day of the week is still referred to as Freya's day – or Friday – in the English language.

The goddess did, however, have a reputation for promiscuity and was said to give herself freely to any of the gods. In myth, she enjoyed an incestuous relationship with Frey, and the divine couple are probably the pair depicted on some tiny gold-foil plaques recovered from Scandinavian sites, which show a man and woman embracing one another.

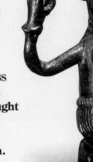

**LOVE GODDESS Figurine of a woman, thought to be Freya, clasping her fertile bosom.**

running parallel with the boundaries. It is not known what crop was to have been sown here, but from other Viking sites it appears that the most widespread cereals were barley, rye and oats. Wheat was much less common, and perhaps restricted to Denmark.

In *Njal's Saga* it is written of a farmer that in spring, 'with a seed basket in one hand and a sword in the other he went out to his cornfield and started to sow.' Enemy raiders and feuding neighbours were among the hardships of the ploughman's life, along with the sullen soils, chill winds and

Nordic drizzle. Yet with a growing season so brief, it was vital to prepare the ground in good time. For ancient peoples throughout northern Europe, the importance of a good harvest is reflected in the religious rites associated with the spring sowing. The Vikings celebrated with rituals dedicated to the fertility god, Frey, at which they called on him for plentiful crops.

The coming of spring allowed families to get out of the longhouse and do a lot of work that winter had prevented. It was perhaps only now, as the sun began to shine, that clothes and blankets could be

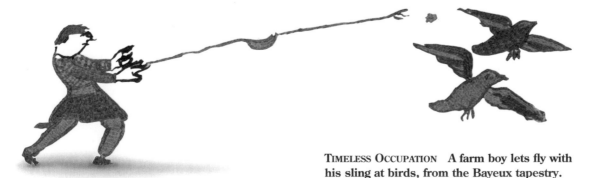

**TIMELESS OCCUPATION   A farm boy lets fly with his sling at birds, from the Bayeux tapestry.**

washed and hung out in the open to dry. While adults tended their fields and their vegetable plots, children fed the pigs and hens, pulled up weeds and chased birds off the growing corn. On most farms, animals were led out of their byres to graze in the fields and meadows around the longhouse. But in Norway, where good farmland was particularly scarce, farmers relied heavily on their herds; and summer was a time when cattle and sheep were moved from the valley farms up to mountain pastures with their unspoilt grazing, which also released more land for crops. There the animals were allowed to range free until the approach of autumn. Norwegian families tending the herds up in the mountains lived in rough shelters of wood or stone.

The spring and summer months were the growing season, when the women and their youngsters tended the burgeoning crops while the men were away. During the early, raiding years of the Viking Age many a Norse farmer took the opportunity to sail westward in search of plunder, returning with treasure and slaves in time to gather in the fruits of the field.

The *Orkneyinga Saga* describes the life of a Norse raider called Svein who would work hard in the spring to get his seed sown. Then, 'when this work was done he would go off and raid the Scottish Isles and Ireland, and he would come home at midsummer. He called this his "spring trip". He would stay at home until the corn had been harvested. Then he

CATTLE FARMING  The stony remains are vestiges of Viking cow-stalls in Greenland. Right: Norse farmers sometimes hung a cowbell around the necks of grazing animals so that livestock could be located with ease.

# A VIKING HERDSMAN

**CHANGELESS SCENE** The landscape of Scandinavia's high mountains has changed little since Viking times.

EINAR AWOKE before dawn and called out to rouse the rest of his family. There were ten of them in the longhouse. Einar's household comprised Astrid, his wife; her sister; three sons and a daughter; a nephew; and two slaves. All now rose with some excitement and prepared themselves for the important day that lay ahead. Stabled in the byre at the end of the dwelling house were two dozen head of cattle and a larger number of sheep, all of which were to be driven today up to the high mountain pasture, where they would remain through the summer. The family had a stone-walled summerhouse, or *shieling*, up in the mountains and five of the household were to go there with the herdsman.

Those who were to leave gathered up the provisions: salt beef in a barrel, sacks of flour, cheeses, barley bread and home-brewed beer, which were loaded onto Einar's horse-drawn cart, along with a small upright loom, an iron cauldron and griddle for cooking, axes for woodchopping, hooks and lines for fishing in the high lakes, and furs and blankets for warmth at night. Then Einar's party said their farewells and drove the livestock out of the byre. A broad, well-worn track led up from the valley floor to the edge of the pine forest, where they took a last look at the farmstead. Then they entered the forest and climbed on upwards. The air grew thinner as they rose higher, and it was late afternoon by the time they reached the high valley and caught sight of the stone-sided longhouse with its simple pens, where they would spend the coming months.

On entering the longhouse they found little had changed since last summer. Einar, however, had reconnoitred the dwelling a week or so before and knew that the roof leaked where the turf had caved in at one end, perhaps under a fall of winter snow. He was already fixing it while the boys penned the herds and unloaded the cart. Astrid, meanwhile lit a fire in the hearth and prepared the evening meal.

ANIMAL WORLD Creatures are engraved on a fragment of bone from the Viking Age.

onset of winter, now was the time to do them. From the pine forests beyond their fields, the farmers of Norway and Sweden brought in the long, straight timbers needed for beams and posts. In Denmark, where conifers were more scarce, farmers brought in oak from the deciduous woodlands, and cut down hazels and willows to weave the wickerwork panels that filled spaces between the upright posts.

The women, meanwhile, brewed beer and stored away the fruits, nuts, vegetables and cheeses that would serve as provisions over the cold months ahead. Fish were preserved by drying: once cleaned and gutted they were slit along the belly, flattened and hung out to dry over a wooden rack. As nights drew in, the Vikings slaughtered many of their animals – especially the older and weaker specimens. The healthiest animals would be fed under cover during the winter, but there was not enough fodder or stabling for the entire herd. Nothing was wasted. While the women preserved the meat by salting, smoking or pickling, farmers tanned the hides to make them into leather.

The onset of winter was celebrated by the Vikings on October 14, with a sacrifice to the gods and entreaties for mild weather. According to the saga-writer Snorri Sturlson, such rites were decreed by no less a figure than the great god Odin himself, when he fixed the customs for all the Nordic peoples: 'There should be a sacrifice at the beginning of winter for a successful year, and at midwinter for a successful regeneration.' The coming ordeal was long and harsh, especially for the

would go raiding again, and not come back until the winter. He called this his "autumn trip".'

Bringing the harvest in safely was, of course, a vital activity, and whole villages would go out with the iron sickles used to cut the corn. The grain was threshed with flails, and after sifting, was stored away in barrels and baskets. Sacrifices were made to the gods in thanksgiving, and before the leaves turned to their autumn colours, villagers combed the countryside for green foliage, which they cut down to make winter fodder using broad-bladed 'leaf knives'.

### ADVENT OF WINTER

Autumn was a time of busy preparation. Farmers chopped wood and stacked it up ready to burn on the fire, and if the longhouse needed any repairs before the

TOOLS OF THE TRADE Chisel, drawknife, axe and bit were among the tools employed by Viking woodworkers for house-building and repairs.

**THRILL OF THE CHASE** A Viking carving from the Isle of Man depicts hunting dogs running after deer.

farmers living in Scandinavia's far north. The Vikings' homeland stretched to a latitude of 71° in northern Norway, well inside the Arctic Circle. Though the climate along Norway's jagged coastland is moderated by the influence of the Gulf Stream, the northern interior is a permafrost zone of mountain and tundra, snowbound for months on end, with temperatures well below freezing. Confined for long nights to the longhouse, farmers must have welcomed the distractions offered by board-games and saga-tellers.

But winter was not a wholly inactive time. While the women continued to cook and to weave, men took the opportunity to repair tools and weapons. Many farmsteads had a furnace, even if this was no more than a hole in the ground, and farmers often forged their own tools, using iron smelted from the local bog ore, which was widespread in the beds of Scandinavian lakes and marshes. Though bog ore was of poor quality by comparison with that mined from rock, it was much more easily obtained as it could be raked up without difficulty. Iron technology reached Scandinavia from central Europe around

500 BC, and the harder metal quickly replaced bronze as the material for most everyday implements. From cooking utensils to battle-axe heads and the nails and rivets used in shipbuilding, iron supplied the Vikings with many essentials.

In winter the Vikings went hunting on skis for wild boar, elk or red deer. From prehistoric times onwards, Scandinavian peoples were using skis, made from lengths of wood up to 6 ft 6 in (2 m) long. Pine was the favoured material, because its natural resins allowed the underside to slide rapidly over ice and snow. For hunters in wetland areas, it was sometimes easier to get around at speed on skis in winter than it was on foot in summer, when the ground was soggy underfoot. The coniferous forests fringing the lakes of Norway and Sweden were the natural habitat of bear, marten, otter and beaver, whose furs were valued for trade.

**WINTER PURSUIT** Viking farmers often went hunting in winter. Snow tracks made their prey easier to follow, and skis offered swift transport over ice-bound terrain.

WOMAN'S TOUCH  A carving on the Oseberg cart shows a woman restraining a swordsman as he strikes at a rider.  Right: Pendant of a woman, possibly a Valkyrie.

wealth and such a large retinue. From this it can be seen what a paragon among women she was.'

Unn's career is followed, like Egil's, into old age. And as death approaches, we observe her taking her favourite grandson, Olaf Feilan, in hand:

'I have been thinking, kinsman, that you ought to establish yourself and take a wife.'

Olaf agrees, and says that he will happily rely on her guidance.

'I have had it in mind,' said Unn, 'that your wedding feast should be held towards the end of this summer, for that is the best time for getting all the necessary provisions; I am sure that our friends will be coming in large numbers, because I intend this to be the last feast I shall hold.'

All speak of a dominant personality: Unn evidently possesses the authority not only to arrange her grandson's marriage but to dispose of her estate in his favour. At the wedding feast she publicly announces that she is giving her house and all her possessions to Olaf. Then, ordering ale to be served to all present, she retires with a stately demeanour to her bedchamber. The drinking goes on all that evening. Next morning Olaf Feilan goes to his grandmother's bedroom. When he enters, Unn is sitting propped up against the pillows; she is dead. Olaf goes back into the hall and announces the news; everyone thinks it most impressive how Unn had kept her dignity to the end.

The feast, which lasts for several days, concludes with Unn's burial in a ship crammed with treasures, under an earthen mound. Archaeologists have excavated several such rich ship-burials in both Scandinavia and other Viking lands. It is interesting that the most splendid of all the burial sites, a grave at Oseberg in Norway, is also the grave of a woman.

### LOVE, MARRIAGE AND DIVORCE

The family was a powerful social unit. As Unn's story reveals, marriages were often arranged by the parents or grandparents, for the alliance was as much between families as between the bride and

groom. Property and reputation were at stake, and the sagas often explore the issues raised by a union. As an institution, moreover, marriage was protected by heavy penalties imposed for illicit liaisons. Adultery was punished by death for the male offender, while the woman was sold into slavery. Promiscuous as they may have been with their concubines and foreign captives, the Vikings took the honour of their own womenfolk very seriously. To compromise a young girl's marriage prospects in any way was punishable; death applied for the rape of virgins.

The wedding itself was clearly an occasion for feasting and brought friends and relations from some distance away. A picture stone, a memorial stone carved with scenes from the event being celebrated, recovered from Alstad in Norway records how one happy bride was brought to her new home: 'Jorun raised this stone after Ol-Arnir married her and took her from west of Ringerike from Ve to Olvestad. Ogmund's stone records it.' A hunting scene, with horses, hounds and falcons accompanies the inscription.

However, it does not seem that in pagan times marriage was necessarily regarded as a lifelong commitment. If a couple wanted a divorce, they had only to inform some witnesses of their readiness to separate. And it says much for the rights of Viking women that in Iceland a wife could, single-handedly, obtain a divorce simply by making a declaration on the grounds of, for example, incompatibility or non consummation of the marriage. Transvestism provided valid grounds, too. The *Laxdaela Saga* tells of a certain Gudrun who obtains a divorce by making her husband wear a low-necked shirt, resembling a woman's blouse. Subsequently her admirer, Thord, divorces his own wife on the grounds that she wears breeches like a man's. Gudrun and Thord then get married and live happily together.

The theme of romantic love crops up repeatedly in the sagas, often in tales of rival suitors who become bitter rivals over the same girl, with murder and mayhem resulting. Of course, these stories

**LOVING COUPLE  A carved stone, or stele, from the Viking Age shows real affection between a couple united in the Christian faith.**

## WARY OF WOMEN

The Vikings showed considerable respect for their womenfolk by the standards of the day. But misogyny — the mistrust of women — was not wholly absent from their culture. The poem known as the *Havamal* advises, 'Do not trust a woman's words, be she single or married; their hearts run on wheels, they are prey to moods.'

were written after the close of the Viking Age and may owe something to the influence of medieval Christianity with its own focus on love as a supreme value in life. Nevertheless, the Norsemen's fondness for women made a strong impression on contemporaries such as Ibn Fadlan and Adam of Bremen, and it is permissible to believe that their interest extended – at least on occasion – to something more than brutish lust.

### 'SHE WAS LOVELY'
Perhaps out of modesty, Viking women often covered their hair with a scarf, cap or hairnet. They also wore a long-sleeved shift, sometimes pleated, with a tunic over the top. Garments were usually made of wool or linen, and the outer tunic was fixed at the shoulders with a pair of bronze brooches, which are among the most common finds at Viking sites.

Often oval in shape, the brooches vary considerably in quality from gilded examples exquisitely decorated with animal patterns, to items produced in quantity from low-grade bronze imprinted with much simpler designs. Strings of coloured beads might be hung between the twin ornaments for decoration, and the brooches served utilitarian purposes too. A number of domestic necessities were often hung from them: knife, purse and comb, as well as the keys that symbolised the authority that women possessed within the house.

Out of doors, Viking women wore a shawl or cloak fixed in front with an ornamental fastening of bronze, silver or gold. This brooch was, typically, circular, rectangular, or trefoil-shaped, for contrast with the oval brooches of the overdress. Women's garments were trimmed with braid in contrasting colours, and the quality of fabric reflected differences in social status. A high-ranking woman wore

# A VIKING BRIDE

THE KISS Stylised images of an embracing couple, possibly deities, on a gold plaque found at Helgo in Sweden.

SIGRID'S PARENTS had arranged the wedding. She was married that morning to Gunulf, son of a warrior chieftain who lived in a valley some distance away, beyond the pine-stacked mountains to the north. Sigrid had met the youth only once before, at a winter feast where she had been placed beside him at the table to discover how they got on. She had found him likable enough – a tall, yellow-haired lad who had found conversation difficult but had frank, open features that promised no harm. When the marriage proposal was raised she left the decision to her father.

Now, however, at the wedding banquet, the fierce-bearded menfolk of Gunulf's family caused her some consternation as they caroused by the light of the hearth fire blazing in her father's hall. Sigrid sat with Gunulf and their parents on a dais at one end of the hall, with embroidered hangings lining the walls behind. Servants had strewn the floor with straw, set out the tables and brought wooden platters of smoked eels and pickled beef to the guests. Sigrid's sisters helped ladle ale from open barrels into the men's drinking horns, and her father's finest Frankish wines were brought out, too. Gunulf's warrior relations had laughed, sung and roared out toasts good-naturedly enough at the outset, but now, as the evening wore on, Sigrid could hear quarrelsome voices raised at the far end of the hall. A drunken taunt was hurled; raw-voiced oaths sworn in reply. Two brawling warriors suddenly upset a table, and knives flashed by the firelight. In the hubbub that followed, Sigrid saw one of the wild-eyed assailants, streaming blood from his forehead, being bundled out of the hall. Gunulf's father motioned his warriors to return to their benches, and the feasting continued.

Later that night a troupe of jugglers entertained the revellers, and a poet regaled them with a myth of the god Frey and his passionate love for Gerd of the White Arms. Sigrid, enjoying the story, found herself becoming intensely irritated with one of the guest warriors who had pulled a bird-bone flute from his cloak and was whistling away tunelessly to himself as the poet declaimed the verses. Suddenly, in a fit of anger, Sigrid rose from the table and called for the warrior to stop. Such behaviour was an insult to the poet, to the god Frey and to her father's hospitality, she declared. The hall was suddenly very quiet and Sigrid – astonished by her own temerity – felt her heart thump with anxiety in case she had spoken out of turn. But Gunulf quickly rose and walked over to the offending warrior, seized the flute and cuffed his head. The man muttered an apology and the poet resumed his tale.

The rest of the evening passed uneventfully. And though Gunulf made no mention of the incident, Sigrid was intensely grateful to him for the support he had shown. She was less anxious, now, about the household she was to enter, knowing that her husband was respected by the warriors and that she herself would not be expected to sacrifice, in marriage, the same right to speak freely that she had enjoyed in her father's house. The wedding feast was not yet over – the celebrations would continue for some days yet, and there were gifts to be exchanged and discussions to be held about property. But as Sigrid retired with Gunulf that night she felt that she could look forward to married life with confidence.

**GLIMMER OF GOLD** The jewellery comes from a Viking-Age grave at Hon near Oslo in Norway. Right: This brooch with pin was probably a dress fastener.

finely woven wool or linen, perhaps quilted with down. Gold thread might be woven into her braided trimmings.

Of Frith, a Norse king's daughter, it is written in the *Saga of the Men of Keelness*: 'She was lovely, and wore a lace-decorated red gown with a thick belt of silver around it. Her plentiful hair was cut like a girl's.' Presumably, the last remark refers to a simple, unadorned style. In adult Viking women, hair was more conventionally worn gathered in a thick knot at the back of the neck. Pale arms, we also know from written sources, were considered particularly beautiful on a woman. Perhaps they distinguished the lady of breeding from the brown-armed field-worker.

Viking men, so often seen gloating over treasure hoards in the sagas, also loved to see their women-folk decked out in splendour. Apart from the brooches, which just about all women wore, wealthier ladies also went about glittering with neck-rings worn as symbols of status. Of Rus women, the Arab emissary

Ibn Fadlan wrote that their neck-rings were carefully valued by the *dirham* (an Islamic coin): 'Round her neck she wears gold or silver rings: when a man collects 10 000 dirhams he gives his wife a neck-ring, when he has 20 000 he gives two rings, and so the wife gets a new ring for each 10 000 dirhams added to the husband's wealth. One woman often has many neck-rings.' Pearl necklaces were other favourite adornments, and crescent-shaped earrings and pendants were imported from the Slavic lands of western Russia and Poland.

The Viking woman of fashion glimmered, too, with the lustre of amber beads, amulets and finger-rings. Amber, an ancient, fossilised tree resin, was a prized commodity of the Nordic regions long before the Viking Age dawned. Back in the Bronze Age, the ancient Greeks and others had obtained supplies from the west coast of Jutland; these resources were exhausted by Viking times, but the Baltic still yielded plentiful quantities. The manufacture of amber jewellery was an important industry in several Viking towns, from Hedeby to York and Dublin. The material could be cut, shaped and polished without much difficulty, as could jet, another popular material for jewellery. Jet is a type of black lignite, a fossilised wood. It was carved to make finger-rings as well as pendants, which were commonly in the form of a coiled snake.

### THE VIKING DANDY

Viking men also wore jewellery. One distinctive item was a braided or twisted arm-ring of silver or gold, often given as a gift by a lord to his favoured retainers. These arm-rings are commonly found in Viking treasure hoards, along with silver bars and coins. The sagas also mention a distinctive ornament known as a

**ADORNMENTS** Arm rings, like these Danish ones, were a characteristic form of ornament.

# CLOTH KIT

NO COMPLETE example of a loom has survived from the Viking Age, but archaeologists have discovered a wealth of the accessories used at every stage of cloth-making. These include spindle whorls which were used for spinning yarn, loom weights, iron combs for carding wool, and cutting shears for the fabric. Housewives often hung small, cylindrical containers, in which they kept their needles and pins of iron or bone, from their brooches.

Fragments of Viking textiles reveal the many different techniques of cloth production in use. One patch of woollen material from Viking York was made in a

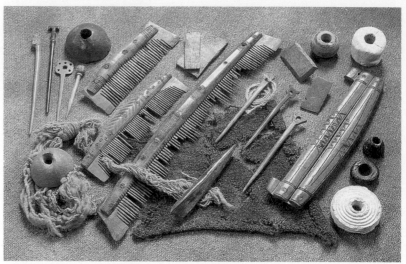

**TEXTILE ACCESSORIES** Bone and antler combs, pins, spindle whorls and woollen cloth from Viking-Age York. Below: The raw materials and textiles are yarn, wool twill, raw wool and tabby silk.

diamond twill pattern, while a 10th-century woollen sock from the same site was made by what is called single-needle knitting, which is still practised in Scandinavia. To make ribbons and decorative edging for the hems of their garments, the Vikings practised tablet-weaving. This technique used rectangular plates of wood or antler, which were perforated at the corners. The weaver passed threads of different colours through the holes, and revolved the plates through 90° or more to create intricate, multi-coloured braids.

*hlad*, which was worn around the forehead. Scholars believe that this was a ribbon made of silk, of a type discovered in a warrior's grave at Mammen, Jutland, decorated in a tendril pattern with gold embroidery.

Beards or drooping moustaches were the rule among men, a fact evident from the texts of the sagas as well as from pictures that have survived from the Viking Age. But the popular notion that the men were completely unkempt is clearly a misconception. The English chronicler, John of Wallingford, describes the Vikings as attractive to women because they bathed on Saturdays, combed their hair and dressed in style. Another English observer rails against the Viking fashions sweeping the Saxon court. Young men, he complained, should not follow the Danish styles of shaved necks and 'blinded eyes' (a likely reference to long fringes). From an Arab merchant, Al-Tartushi, it is learnt that Norsemen, as well as women, sometimes used eye make-up.

In pictures from the Viking era, Norsemen are sometimes shown wearing a pointed or round-topped cap. Male bodywear included a belted tunic, sometimes worn with an undershirt, and a long, heavyweight cloak fastened with a brooch over the right shoulder to keep the sword-arm free. Furs

## TOGGLE TOYS

Certain objects, known as 'toggles', have puzzled archaeologists in Viking York. Made from particular pig bones (the axial metapodials) they were once thought to be dress fasteners or bobbins for textile manufacture. However, they show no signs of the wear or polish that might be expected from such uses. A popular suggestion today is that the toggles were toys, threaded onto a twisted cord that was pulled to make them spin and hum.

were used to trim the cloak, which was a stately garment, conferring considerable dignity on the wearer. Trousers, however, came in a marvellous variety of dandyish styles: narrow, drainpipe types, calf-length bell bottoms and huge, 'plus-four' breeches bound tight below the knee with 'puttee'-style strips of cloth. Baggy trousers are depicted in a famous woven tapestry recovered from the Oseberg ship in south Norway and on carved stones from Gotland, while the 10th-century Arab traveller and geographer, Ibn Rustah, writes of the Rus traders that they wore exaggeratedly full trousers gathered at the knees.

This, evidently, was not a rare freak of fashion but a widespread style that lasted throughout the Viking era. The skin-tight drainpipes were similarly popular. They, too, are shown on the Oseberg tapestry, while a saga-writer refers to the problems they could cause: 'Snorri's servant tried to pull off the wounded man's trousers and grumbled, "They weren't lying when they said that you sons of

Thorbrand are vain, your breeches are so tight that I can't pull them off".'

Clothes varied considerably in cut: loose-fitting tunics and trousers were obviously better suited to everyday work, but there is plentiful evidence of careful tailoring in upper-class menswear. And from the Viking site at Birka in Sweden come some remarkable examples of Oriental influence. Splendidly furnished graves there have yielded pieces of jackets cut much like kaftans, buttoned or belted, with silk borders and gold-thread ornamentation. The jackets, which came with matching headgear, were evidently all the rage among the fashionable rich in a trading town that did business with Asian merchants. And the materials must have come from far afield, for the secrets of silk manufacture were not yet known in northern Europe. Though knowledge of silk-making had spread beyond its Chinese origins it was still

HOLDING THE BABY Viking women generally wore their hair covered. The tunic fixed with brooches over a long-sleeved shift is typical.

EYEWITNESS

# 'THEY ARE LOUSY AS DONKEYS'

IBN FADLAN, THE 10th-century Arab emissary, described the ablutions of Viking traders on the Volga. His judgment is that of a fastidious Muslim, required by his religion to perform careful ablutions five times a day.

❧ They are the filthiest of God's creatures. They do not wash after discharging their natural functions, neither do they wash their hands after meals. They are lousy as donkeys ... They wash their hands and faces every day in incredibly filthy water. Every morning the girl brings her master a large bowl of water in which he washes his hands and face and hair, then blows his nose into it and spits into it. When he has finished the girl takes the bowl to his neighbour who repeats the performance. Thus the bowl goes the rounds of the entire household. ❧

49

**VIKING OF KIEV** The belted tunic, cloak and baggy breeches were characteristic of Norsemen everywhere.

also wore ankle-length or taller boots. In Viking footwear the single, flat-piece sole – without a heel – was usually of cattle hide, and goatskin often furnished the material for the uppers, which were sometimes coloured. When the sole was worn it was often discarded and replaced with a new one. At the Viking dig in York discarded soles are much more often found than complete shoes.

### WOODEN WEAPONS, MODEL BOATS

No examples of children's clothing exist, but it is fair to assume that youngsters went clad much like their parents. A Viking's childhood passed quickly, for sons and daughters worked alongside their parents from an early age. Boys would learn to plough a straight furrow, cut wood with an adze, stoke the fire at the smithy. Girls would milk the cows, make butter, spin and weave at the loom. Huddled around the longhouse hearth, children would listen to the riddles, poems, tales of gods and ancestors, that formed the shared culture of their kinsfolk. And they played with toys, too: wooden weapons, carved animals and model boats have been recovered from some Viking sites.

The Vikings were clearly fond of their children, and particularly liked to see evidence of manliness in a boy; a certain independence of spirit was valued more highly than meek obedience. Yet the Norsemen were also capable of some callousness with regard to their offspring. No rune stones, stones bearing inscriptions carved in the runic alphabet, were carved in memory of children, and very few were given a formal burial. Before the coming of Christianity in the 10th century, moreover, unwanted babies would be taken out to a forest glade or hillside and left to die of exposure.

More often, though, the birth of a child would be a welcome event. In a ceremony resembling Christian baptism, water was sprinkled on the baby and a name was chosen for him or her. The three stern spirits known as the Norns, goddesses of Fate, were believed to watch over the birth,

confined to Byzantium, the Near East, North Africa and southern Spain.

Clues to the finery of the upper classes have been found in Scandinavia's rich grave sites. And some bundles of cast-off clothing, discovered in the mud of Hedeby harbour, have provided comparative examples of the type and quality of fabric available at different levels of society. These came mostly in the form of scraps, probably used as a packing material or as brushes for tarring ships, and include fragments of a long, tight-fitting dress and part of a pair of men's plus fours finely woven from wool in two colours.

In contrast to the scarcity of woven garments, examples of footgear are abundant. From these it is evident that Viking men and women commonly wore low-cut leather shoes of the slip-on type. Men

**LEATHER FOOTGEAR** The Vikings wore slip-on shoes and taller boots. The soles, which had no heel, could be replaced.

# THE IMPORTANCE OF GOOD GROOMING

A CELEBRATED late 9th-century Viking named Harald, son of Halfdan the Black, once made a solemn vow that he would not have his hair combed or cut until he was the sole king in Norway.

As Harald's hair grew longer and more untidy, he was dubbed Shaggy Harald. However, after many a battle he was finally able to redeem his vow: the scissors came out, he was properly coiffed, and his name was changed to Harald Finehair.

The implication of this story is that – despite popular belief in Viking uncouthness – it was quite unusual for a Viking lord to go about looking unkempt. And the evidence of archaeology confirms that ordinary people, too, were properly concerned with hair care. A very common find at Viking sites is the single-sided comb, sometimes in its own comb-case. The comb itself was typically made from the antler of red deer, a material easily gathered after the yearly spring shedding, and well suited to the makers' purpose. Antler is both stronger and more flexible than, for example, bone, and its natural advantages were enhanced by cutting the parts along the antler 'grain'. The comb came in three pieces, the middle one strengthened by two riveted to either side. The teeth were formed by sawing into the central plate.

Grooming was not merely cosmetic. The abundance of combs probably owes much to people's desire to rid themselves of the itching lice and fleas that archaeological research has revealed to have been a problem in Viking homes.

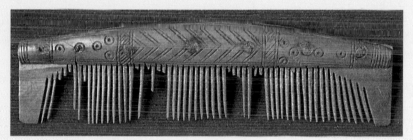

**ANTLER COMB** Despite their reputation, the Vikings appear to have been surprisingly well groomed.

and much thought was given to the right choice of name. It was believed that some of the good luck and worthy qualities of a hero or exalted kinsman might pass on to the child who received his name. In the sagas, when a son is born to Ragnar Lodbrok, the son of Sigurd Hring, the mother bids the maidservants carry the child to the hall where Ragnar takes his little son in his arms, and folds his cloak around him. When asked what name should be given, Ragnar says:

*Sigurd shall the boy be named;*
*He will fight battles,*
*And be much like his mother,*
*And be called his father's son;*
*He will be called foremost*
*Of Odin's line.*

The gods supplied several common names, and those based on the god Thor were particular favourites. Thorstein, Thorfinn, Thorvald, Toke and Thorkel were just a few examples for boys, while for girls Thora was a popular choice and one that has survived into the 20th century. Other common names were derived from powerful animals, such as Bjorn (bear), Orm (snake) and Ulf (wolf). They were sometimes used in a combination such as Ulfbjorn, as if to double the potency of the name.

The Vikings did not make use of surnames in the modern sense. Children simply adapted their father's first name, so that Erik, son of Magnus, became Erik Magnusson; Erik's son Knud became Knud Eriksson. To read the sagas is to encounter a fantastic pageant of personalities. Eirik Bloodaxe, Harald Bluetooth, Ivar the Boneless, Bue the Fat, Ulf the Unwashed, Einar the Bellyshaker ... these and many other evocative nicknames demonstrate what a keen eye the Scandinavians had for quirks and oddities of character. However, there is no evidence that the people in question were known by

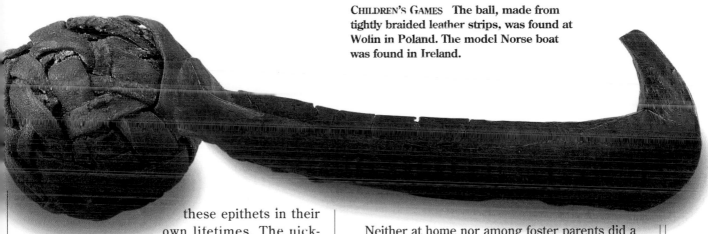

CHILDREN'S GAMES  The ball, made from tightly braided leather strips, was found at Wolin in Poland. The model Norse boat was found in Ireland.

these epithets in their own lifetimes. The nick-names may have been invented by the storytellers to lend colour to their tales.

### 'WHY SHOULD I REAR THIS BABE?'

Not every youngster spent the whole of his or her childhood in the longhouse where he was born. It was a practice among the Vikings to hand over their children to friends or kinsfolk of slightly lower status than themselves, to be brought up and taught the necessary accomplishments of life. In accepting the role of childminder and tutor, a Viking family acknowledged that they ranked lower in society than the true parents. The sagas illustrate the fact in the tale of a trick played on the 10th-century English king, Athelstan, by Norway's king, Harald Finehair (the two rulers were reputed to be on good terms). Harald has a friend place a Norwegian child of royal blood on the English king's knee and demand that the monarch bring it up. 'Why should I rear this babe, though he were the son of Harald and his queen?' queries Athelstan.

'You have had this child upon your knee; you are therefore his foster-father,' comes the reply. 'You may kill him if you will, but with him you cannot kill all the sons of Harald, and it will be said hereafter, as it has ever been said, that he who fosters the child of another is the lesser man.' (The episode was a practical joke to repay a similar trick Athelstan had once played on Harald, and the English king has the child raised at his court.)

VIKING TOYS  Children's games were only for infants. By the time they reached the age of seven, most youngsters would be working alongside their parents.

Neither at home nor among foster parents did a Viking child undergo formal schooling. Bodily prowess was much more important to the ordinary Norseman than intellectual achievement: learning to swim, row, wrestle and wield a sword were the priorities for any aspiring warrior. Nonetheless, such noble skills as composing poetry and writing in runes must have required careful tuition, and it would be some time before the young Viking could say, with Earl Rognvald in the *Orkneyinga Saga*:

> *I'm a master of draughts*
> *And of nine kinds of sport.*
> *I am skilled at runes,*
> *And in letters a scholar.*
> *Glide I on ski,*
> *Shoot and row well enough,*
> *Play the harp and make verses*
> *Or toil in the smithy.*

Mothers, fathers, sons and daughters, all united by tight bonds of kinship, nevertheless had to operate in a society that extended far beyond

### WOMEN WARRIORS?

Did Norse women fight alongside their menfolk in battle? Certain medieval Irish texts do mention female Viking warriors. However, these are likely to have been fictional. It is known that some women crossed the Channel when a large Danish army invaded England around 890, but they were wives who were hoping to settle. Texts mention that efforts were made to move them with their children to places of safety when the fighting commenced.

HARD STARE  Carved ivory pieces from the 12th-century chess set found on the Isle of Lewis.

seat pillars. Sometimes at a feast, however, guests drew lots to decide the seating, and if a young man repeatedly drew a place next to the same girl, it was thought that the gods favoured a marriage.

While the servants and cupbearers replenished guests with beer, mead and imported wine, poets known as *scalds* declaimed stories of the great. Jugglers and acrobats might also entertain the throng,

and music was supplied by bone flute, panpipes and lyre. In one text the type of musician called upon to play at a drinking session is disparaged as an 'ale minstrel'. But the feast was much more than an opportunity for heavy drinking. Gifts were exchanged, alliances sealed and sacrifices made to the gods. A great feast might last for several days, and enhance the host's prestige as a man of wealth

## MUSICAL INSTRUMENTS

To JUDGE from archaeological finds, bone flutes were the most widespread instruments among the Vikings. They were often made from kitchen leftovers: the wings of geese, swans or cranes, or from the shinbones of sheep. Naturally hollow, they required little more than trimming and perforation with a knife, though a small block was also needed to narrow the mouthpiece.

(The Viking 'flute' in fact resembled the modern recorder, in that it was blown through the end.)

Panpipes were made by boring a row of holes into a thin, flat piece of wood. Open only at one end, the holes varied in length so that different notes could be obtained without the complication of fingering. Study of the notes produced by the panpipes shows that the Vikings used something

resembling the modern major scale in music. The same scale is used in 10th-century instructions for tuning a lyre – another instrument known to the Vikings. Several Norse lyres have been discovered by archaeologists, usually in fragments, which betray their fragile construction. The lyre was a particularly suitable instrument for the songs sung by poets in praise of gods and heroes.

BONE FLUTE  The instrument is carved from the hollow bone of a bird.

and generous spirit. The most lavish were remembered for generations; the *Laxdaela Saga* reports that the biggest ever held in Iceland was a funeral feast given for one of the original settlers, Hjalti Thordarson, by his two sons. The guests there numbered about 1440 people.

### CHECKMATE

For quieter entertainment in their spare time, the Vikings had board games. One in particular, called *hnefatafl*, is often referred to in the sagas. Though the rules are not known, several wooden boards and playing pieces, have been recovered from archaeological sites. *Hnefatafl* was a game of skill for two players who had unequal numbers of counters. The purpose was for the large army to drive a king with a smaller army into a corner of the board. A particularly well-preserved board, probably for *hnefatafl*, was discovered at Ballinderry in Ireland. This was an Irish settlement rather than a Viking one, but the board is of Scandinavian design and made around the 10th century. It comprises a decorated square with seven rows of seven peg-holes, a marked centre and marked corner holes. The board owes its fine state of preservation to the cold and waterlogged lakeside site in which it was embalmed.

Other such games were known, including one very similar to nine-men's-morris, a board game in which two players try to manoeuvre their pieces into a winning formation, and this is probably what is being played on an 11th-century Swedish rune stone showing two men 'at board'. A multitude of gaming pieces – of glass, walrus ivory, antler, stone and wood – have turned up at Viking sites, sometimes as grave goods in burials. And the Norsemen obviously enjoyed gambling with dice to judge by the number of bone dice also recovered.

At the end of the Viking era, a new craze had begun to sweep Scandinavia. This was chess, which is thought to have originated in India around AD 500 and quickly spread to neighbouring Persia, where it acquired many now-familiar names and terms. (The expression 'checkmate' derives from the Persian word *shamat*, meaning 'the king is helpless'.) It was presumably through their Arab contacts that the Vikings acquired a taste for the Persian war game. Superb Norse chessmen, carved from walrus ivory, have been recovered from the Isle of Lewis in the Hebrides; dating from the 12th century, they make up what is thought to be the oldest complete chess set in existence. And chess also features in the sagas. The 13th-century *Heimskringla* tells how the Danish king Canute sits down to a match with his kinsman Ulf. Canute makes a bad move, losing a knight, and wants to take it again. Ulf contemptuously abandons the game but pays dearly for his lack of deference; he is later found stabbed to death in a church, on the orders of the king.

## ICE-SKATING AMONG THE VIKINGS

SIMPLE ICE SKATES are common finds at Viking sites, and are referred to in written sources as 'ice-legs'. They were usually made from a horse's foot bone – the metapodial – though similarly shaped cattle bones have been found, too. Smoothed flat on the underside, the bone was sometimes drilled through to make a hole for a footstrap. The wearer gained momentum by levering himself or herself along the ice with a sharpened stick something like a modern ski-pole. Skates offered a means of winter transport over Scandinavia's frozen lakes, rivers and marshes and may well have been used for leisure too. In 12th-century London, youths held mock tournaments on the frozen Thames, jousting with their skate poles, and it is easy to believe that the Vikings relished similar games.

**WINTER WEAR  A Viking's leather boot on an ice skate made from animal bone.**

# VIKING
# EXPANSION

Terror came to foreign shores when the Vikings took to their longships. This medieval
stained glass from Canterbury Cathedral, England, depicts the Danes' sack
of the city in AD 1011. The invaders captured the archbishop, and killed him when he
refused to let himself be ransomed. The *Anglo-Saxon Chronicle* records how, drunk on
wine, the invaders pelted the churchman with bones and heads of cattle before
crushing his skull with the back of an axe, and so 'sent his holy soul to God's kingdom'.

# THE NORSE ONSLAUGHT

For well over two centuries, pagan pirates swarmed in their dragon ships out of Scandinavia

to ravage the undefended monasteries and settlements of western Europe. Nothing,

it seemed, could slake the Vikings' thirst for silver and slaves.

ON A STORMY night 1000 years ago, an Irish monk jotted the following verse in the margin of a book:

*The wind is bitter tonight*
*It tosses the sea's white hair*
*I have no fear that fierce raiders*
*Will sail the seas on such a night.*

Those raiders were, of course, the Vikings. The onslaughts on Britain began in 793 with a violent assault on the Holy Island of Lindisfarne, just off the north-eastern shore of England. A centre of learning and literature where craftsmen produced some of the masterworks of Anglo-Saxon art, Lindisfarne's monastery had been built in an exposed coastal position in the belief that it would be invulnerable from the sea. To the cultured brethren who nurtured Christianity in Britain, the attack seemed a hellish visitation, and in the *Anglo-Saxon Chronicle*, an account of Anglo-Saxon and Viking England compiled in the late 9th century, it was described with supernatural embellishments, as if it were an act of Judgment: 'In this year [793] terrible signs

**HOLY ISLAND**  An aerial view of Lindisfarne, a cradle of Christianity in England, whose attack by Vikings in 793 heralded a whirlwind of raids.

## THE LINDISFARNE RAID

THE FIRST VIKING raid to be recorded in documents was the attack on the monastery on Lindisfarne in 793. The shock caused by this event was evidently widespread, for several different accounts have survived. Among them was this description, written by the monk and chronicler of medieval England, Simeon of Durham: ❛ And they came to the church of

MEN OF WAR A 9th-century stone from Lindisfarne may show the raid.

Lindisfarne, laid everything to waste with grievous plundering, trampled the holy places with polluted feet, dug up the altars and seized all the treasures of the holy church. They killed some of the brothers; some they took away with them in fetters; many they drove out, naked and loaded with insults; and some they drowned in the sea. ❜

appeared over Northumbria and greatly frightened the inhabitants. There were immense whirlwinds and exceptional flashes of lightning, and fiery dragons were seen flying in the air. A great famine followed soon upon these portents, and a little after that, on 8th June, the ravages of the heathen destroyed God's church on Lindisfarne, bringing rapine and slaughter.'

News of the pagan onslaught sent waves of horror and alarm spreading through Europe. Nor was it forgotten locally. Many years ago, archaeologists at the Lindisfarne site recovered a 11th-century

HALLOWED RUINS  The soaring 'rainbow arch' can be seen in the centre of the skeletal remains of Lindisfarne's priory church.

carved stone that has been taken to depict the raid: on one side is a wild procession of seven warriors in heavy jerkins and narrow trousers, wielding swords and axes overhead. Cartoon-like in its crude vigour, the scene communicates an unmistakable sense of menace. Scholars today believe that the so-called Lindisfarne Stone was a grave-marker rather than a commemorative monument. Nonetheless, it dates from not long after the raid, and even if it does not depict the actual attack, it certainly captures the war-like spirit in which it was carried out.

The Lindisfarne raid was only the beginning.

Over the next few years the Vikings struck at other treasure-rich and undefended monasteries and abbeys. Wearmouth and Jarrow on the north-east coast were burned in 794. In 795, the Norsemen attacked Rathlin Island off Ireland. In the same year, St Columba's monastery at Iona succumbed to the Norse fury – and it was to fall victim again in 802 and 806. In 797 it was the turn of Kintyre in Scotland and the shrine of St Patrick on the Isle of Man.

In 799, moreover, the dragon-prowed longships and fierce-bearded raiders were reported at islands off the French coast. At this time France and much of mainland Europe were governed by the mighty Charlemagne, and as long as the Frankish emperor reigned, the Norsemen dared only make hit-and-run raids on his lands. But when Charlemagne died in 814 his realm began to fall apart, leaving vast territories prey to the seaborne warriors. The Vikings sailed up the great rivers of Europe, killing and pillaging over large areas deep inland. Paris, Hamburg, Lisbon, Cadiz and Pisa fell victim to the Norsemen, whose terror lasted, on and off, for 200 years.

For Norse raiders, the great enabler was the longship – a supreme achievement of Dark-Age technology. The Scandinavians' heavy reliance on waterborne travel required a high degree of ship-building skill, which they probably developed while constructing smaller ferries and fishing smacks for Scandinavia's countless fiords, rivers and bays. The Roman writer, Tacitus, provided a brief description of Nordic vessels as early as AD 98, indicating that they were at this time only rowing boats, presumably incapable of ocean travel: 'The Northern ships differ from the normal in having a prow at both ends. They do not rig sails. Their oars are loosely fitted and can be moved from one side to the other if necessary.'

Masts and sails, thought to have been added during the 8th century, obviously provided the means to venture further afield. It seems, however, that even before this time Norse seamen were rowing

FACE OF FURY  A dragon head carved on a wooden post was found among the relics in the Oseberg ship.

NORSE FLEET  The prows of ships are incised in wood. An inscription reads, 'Here goes the Sea-Darer'.

across the North Sea to reach English shores, for there is strong evidence of contact between Britain and Scandinavia before the great longships were developed. Various objects have been recovered, in particular from the famous ship burial at Sutton Hoo in East Anglia, that closely resemble artefacts from contemporary sites in Sweden. The Sutton Hoo grave is that of an Anglo-Saxon king who was buried at some date between 625 and 660. His shield and magnificent helmet – symbol of a pagan warrior aristocrat – belong to the Scandinavian cultural tradition.

Sail-power in the 8th century gave a dramatic impetus to Scandinavian expansion. And though the 793 attack on Lindisfarne is the first recorded raid, written sources hint at increased overseas activity just beforehand. For example, the *Anglo-Saxon Chronicle* for the year 789 reports that three Scandinavian ships arrived at Portland in Wessex, possibly on a trading mission, and that an incident took place there during which an English royal officer

was killed. In 792, King Offa of Mercia sent out a message for warriors to defend the south coast against a threat from pagan raiders who may have been Vikings.

### THE DRAGON SHIPS

In the onslaughts that followed the Lindisfarne attack, the longships freighted the dread barbarians across the face of Christendom and beyond. They were long, light and slender vessels, propelled by a square sail and oars, with a large steering oar situated on the right-hand side near the stern. The steering gear was sophisticated, the great oar being fixed to starboard by an axle so that the helmsman had only to push and pull on a tiller to change direction.

Many surviving longships are constructed from oak and are clinker built: the hull is made from overlapping planks known as *strakes*, which were nailed together and lashed to the hull. As the frame was not rigidly fixed to the planks, it was able to

# THE GOKSTAD SHIP

Excavations at Scandinavian burial mounds have revealed the grandeur and elegance of Norse ships, and none is more breathtaking than the Gokstad ship found in 1880 at a burial mound in south-western Norway. Now on display at the Viking Ship Museum in Bygdoy near Oslo, the Gokstad ship measures 76 ft 6 in (23.3 m) from prow to stern and is 17 ft 3 in (5.25 m) wide amidships. The hull weighs over 7 tons, yet the vessel sat lightly on the waves: even allowing for an additional 10 tons of crewmen and freight it drew only about 3 ft (1 m) of water.

The Gokstad ship was built around AD 850, and some years later was brought ashore to furnish a dead king with his funeral abode. The monarch, who died in his 50s, was laid on a bed within the ship, accompanied by his weapons, possessions and an assortment of sacrificed animals, among them horses and dogs. These would have been included to provide the king with transport and companionship on his journey to the next world, and may also have served as offerings to the gods.

The ship was found in a trench dug into the local blue clay, and mourners had heaped more clay over it to form a high, oval mound. The blue clay had protected the ship from the decaying effects of air contact, and the vessel had survived in an excellent state of preservation.

Superbly crafted, the Gokstad ship was built chiefly of oak, with a thick pine mast and a large sail carried on a single yard 36 ft (11 m) long. The sail was made from pieces of red and white woollen cloth stitched together in a double thickness to create a striped or chequered appearance.

Like other Viking craft, the Gokstad ship was clinker-built (with overlapping wedge-shaped planks), and the planks were lashed to the vessel's slender ribs by pliable spruce roots – an arrangement that gave it a supple structure allowing it to withstand the buffeting of the waves. There were 16 oar-ports on each side and 32 oars made to different lengths so that all would reach the water at the same time.

The ship was found with 64 shields tied to battens along its sides. The number of shields – twice that of the oar-ports – suggests a double crew, which allowed for rowing in shifts. Each shield overlapped the next, creating an alternating yellow and black pattern – the visual effect must have been dazzling.

The remains of three rowing boats, spars, an anchor and a pine gangplank with cut-out steps in its top side and a pole at one end for securing it were also found with the ship, as were the gabled ends of a tent that was probably erected alongside the ship when it was moored to the land, the timbers carved with animal heads to scare evil spirits away from the sleepers.

As early as 1893, a replica of the Gokstad ship was built and sailed from Norway to North America. Captain Magnus Andersen, who sailed the replica ship to America, wrote of the 10 ft (3 m) oak rudder, shaped like the blade of a giant oar, as a work of genius – 'a man could steer with this tiller in all kinds of weather'. The supple keel, moreover, withstood the worst pounding of storm waves, and though heavy seas might cause the gunwales to twist out of true by as much as 6 in (15 cm) they did not snap under the strain.

**DANGEROUS CURVES**
**The predatory elegance of Viking craft is revealed in the hull of the Gokstad ship.**

bend slightly in rough seas instead of breaking up.

One of the great advances in ship design over Iron-Age vessels was the long, deep keel shaped from a single piece of wood. The keel may have been introduced at the same time as sail-power – in order to support a tall, heavy mast something sturdier was needed than a piece of bottom-planking. In the Viking longship, the mast fitted into a massive block of wood, called the mastfish, which rested on the keel, and could be raised and lowered even when the ship was moving.

The keel also provided the ship with a backbone strong enough to resist the considerable pressure exerted by the water. Timbers were shaped so that their grain followed the shape of the component being made in order to exploit the wood's natural strength and flexibility. The serpentine elasticity in the hull was a tremendous advantage, allowing the whole to give with the impact of stormy seas while remaining completely watertight.

Low and narrow, the Viking warship was a predator built for speed and capable of 10 knots or more under sail. The mast could be lowered for surprise attacks, or to manoeuvre under low bridges and overhanging trees when navigating up rivers deep inland. The smaller longships were also light enough to be carried overland by their crew, called a portage, if rapids and rocks presented a problem, or if it was necessary to leave one waterway and continue on another.

The ship's main purpose was to carry warriors to the scene of a land attack. Battles at sea were not particularly common, so the speedy longship did not need the encumbrance of heavy wooden fortifications. Nonetheless, naval engagements did sometimes occur, and typically began with the attackers showering missiles on their opponents before closing in, boarding their ship and engaging in hand-to-hand fighting. The biggest maritime engagements were between Scandinavians, and the most famous was the Battle of Svold, fought in about 1000. In this epic encounter,

**GLITTERING DISCOVERY**

Some Viking treasure hoards have come to light in remarkable circumstances. In 1858, a cache of some 90 silver artefacts – coins, ingots, neck-rings and brooches – was found near the beach of Skaill Bay in Orkney. Weighing more than 15 lb (7 kg), the hoard was found by a boy out rabbit-hunting. It had been uncovered by burrowing rabbits.

King Olaf Tryggvason of Norway perished while doing battle with an alliance of the Swedes and Danes.

Fast, efficient and versatile, Norse longships thrilled their makers with their beauty – the Vikings clearly derived immense aesthetic satisfaction from their perfect lines. In some examples, prow and stern curved elegantly up to ends carved with snarling dragon heads, or adorned with glittering metalwork. Poets sang the vessels' praises as 'steeds of the waves', and gave them names such as *Wave Walker*, *Sea Bird*, *Raven of the Wind* and *Ocean-striding Bison*.

The author of *King Harald's Saga* relished the dread that the longship inspired in its victims:

> *Men will quake with terror*
> *Ere the seventy sea-oars*
> *Gain their well-earned respite*
> *From the labours of the ocean.*
> *Norwegian arms are driving*
> *This iron-studded dragon*
> *Down the storm-tossed river,*
> *Like an eagle with wings beating.*

A similar enthusiasm was displayed by the hero of *Egil's Saga,* who in boyhood proclaimed:

> *My mother once told me*
> *She'd buy me a longship,*
> *A handsome oared vessel*
> *To go sailing with Vikings:*
> *To stand at the stern-post*
> *And steer a fine warship,*
> *Then head back for harbour*
> *And hew down some foemen.*

By contrast, the imagery of the poet Arnor is almost beatific. In writing about King Magnus the
*continued on page 73*

# THE VIKING SHIPWRIGHT

Longships and merchant ships had the same general features, but the final result depended on the judgment of the shipwright.

ACCORDING TO the sagas, the biggest ship ever built by the Vikings was the *Long Serpent*, constructed at Trondheim in 998 for King Olaf Tryggvason of Norway. It had 68 oars (compared to Gokstad's 32) and could carry over 200 warriors. The keel was 118 ft (36 m) long, and bows and stern were covered with beaten gold.

Snorri Sturlson, the poet, tells the story of its construction in Heimskringla. The shipwright was a man called Thorberg the Trimmer, 'but there were many others involved, some to do the planking, some to trim the wood, some to make rivets, some to carry timber; and all the materials used in the construction were very carefully chosen. The ship was both long and broad and high-sided, and stoutly timbered.

'While they were putting on the planks, it so happened that Thorberg had to go home to his farm on urgent business; by the time he came back, the ship was planked up on both sides. That same evening the king went to see how the vessel looked, along with

Thorberg and others, and everybody said that never had such a large and handsome longship been seen before.'

No shipbuilding yard of the Norse era has yet been found, though archaeologists have discovered places where vessels underwent repairs. Traces of a 'dry' dock – where water could be drained out of the dock so that a ship's underside could be worked on – have even been located at Paviken on the island of Gotland. Besides great vessels like those found at Gokstad and Oseberg, many tools and countless iron rivets have also survived from the Viking Age, so that it is possible to build up a clear picture of how the Norse shipwright went about his business.

1. The long, T-shaped keel was laid down first.

2. The overlapping planks, or strakes, were nailed together to form the sides of the ship.

3. Loops on the inside of the strakes tied the sides of the ship to ribs fixed to the keel, and the bottom row of planks was then nailed to the keel.

4. Wooden crossbeams called knees were stretched across the width of the ship and nailed in place in order to strengthen the framework.

5. Oar-ports were bored in the sides of the ship, and wooden covers that swivelled on a nail were

sometimes added to stop leakage when the ship was under sail.

6. Planking was laid for the deck. As the planks were laid, the ship was caulked with animal hair or wool yarn, and tar was applied between the strakes to seal any gaps. The sides were covered with tar to make them watertight.

The Viking shipwright did not work from plans, but relied on rule of thumb and his own experience and judgment of the optimum ratios of length to breadth to depth for different types of ships. A longship, which was required to be fast, would be much narrower for its length than a merchant ship, which would be broader and deeper in order to accommodate cargo.

WOODCUTTERS  Men fell trees for ships' timbers, in a scene from the Bayeux tapestry.

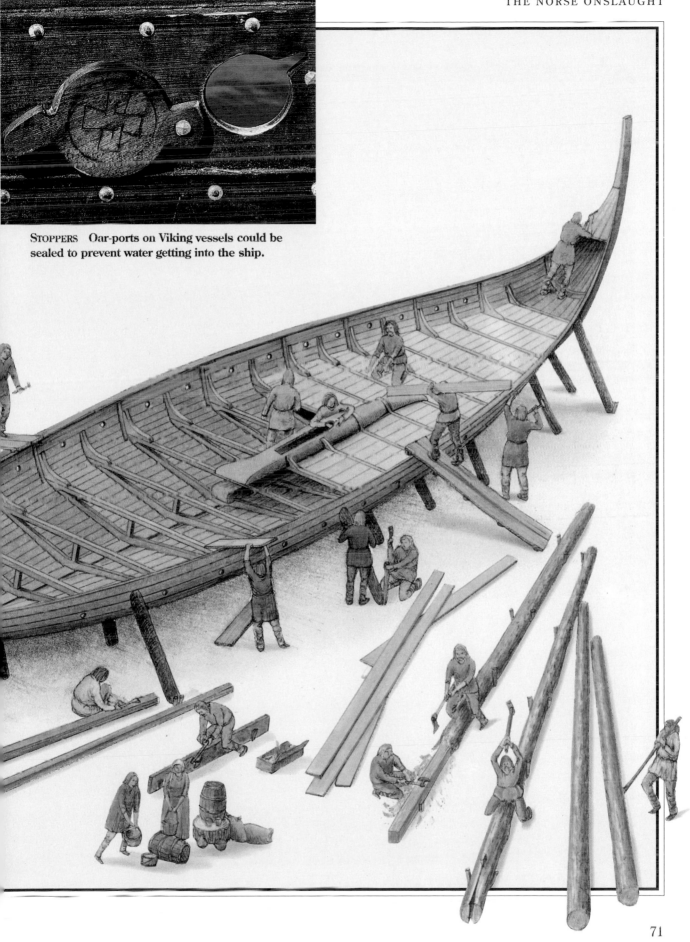

**STOPPERS** Oar-ports on Viking vessels could be sealed to prevent water getting into the ship.

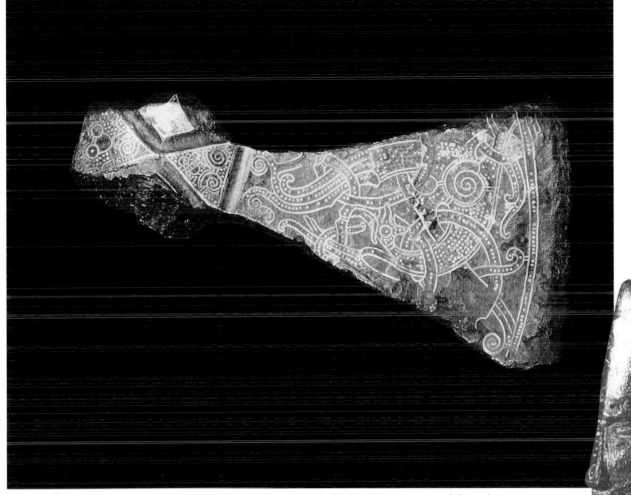

**CUTTING EDGE** Inlaid silver embellishes the iron head of this 10th-century ceremonial axe from Mammen, Jutland. Right: A Viking head, with a conical helmet, carved from elk antler.

and swordsmen slashed at opponents rather than stabbing. The traditional fighting style apparently required skill. 'In the old days when men fought in battle,' it is reported, 'they did not strike fast and furiously, but took their time and picked their strokes carefully so that they were few but terrible. More regard was given to the weight of each blow than to the number struck.'

By comparison with the multitude of swords found at Viking sites, the number of axes found is relatively low. Yet the battle-axe was, in many ways, the most characteristic weapon of the Vikings, and is recalled in the name of one of the most famous Viking kings, Eirik Bloodaxe – so called because he slaughtered his way to the throne through a multitude of half-brothers and rival claimants. The axe was used by the earliest Scandinavian farmer warriors for fighting and chopping timber alike. A typical example consisted of a wooden shaft some 4 ft (1.2 m) long, with a large curved blade slotted on and wedged tight at the top. As with the sword, the cutting edge was of a specially hardened metal welded onto the rest of the blade. Most battle-axes discovered by archaeologists were plain in appearance, and can only be distinguished from everyday tools by the fact that they were found in warriors' graves. Nonetheless, a handful of decorated types have been found, and one especially fine example from a noble burial at Mammen in Jutland is so beautifully inlaid with silver that it has given its name to a whole trend in adornment – the Mammen Style of Viking art.

The decorative battle-axe was, however, a status symbol used chiefly for ceremony and display. The

**PENETRATOR  The blade of a bronze Viking spearhead, found in Sweden.**

more brutal uses to which an axe could be put are vividly evoked in a passage from *Njal's Saga*. 'Skarp-Hedin raced down to the river, axe in hand. On the far side of the river, the ice had formed a slight mound, which was as slippery as glass. On this mound stood Thrain and his men. Skarp-Hedin gathered himself and sprang straight across the river, steadied himself on landing and slid on, skimming along the ice like a bird. Just as Thrain was putting on his helmet, Skarp-Hedin swept up to him. He swung the axe and crashed it down on Thrain's head splitting it down to the jaws and spilling his back teeth onto the ice.'

### THE 'SERPENT OF THE BATTLE'

For close combat, the Vikings used short, single-edged daggers. Heavy spears for thrusting and lighter javelins for throwing were other key items in the warrior's kit. Spears had slender, tapering blades of iron and, though rarely decorated, nevertheless acquired names such as 'serpent of the battle' and 'flying dragon of the wounds', which indicate the esteem in which they were held. The bow and arrow – a favourite hunting weapon – was also used in battle. Many Viking arrowheads have survived in a multitude of shapes – barbed, spiky or leaf-shaped – and when fitted to modern shafts prove to have great penetrating power. The original bows, like the arrow shafts, were made of wood and have generally been lost through decay. Nonetheless, one well-preserved bow was discovered at Hedeby; over 6 ft (1.8 m) long and made of yew, it is not unlike larger examples of the long-bows that English archers made famous in the Middle Ages.

Warriors carried large, round, wooden shields strengthened by an iron disc at the centre. Some were covered with leather with an iron band around the rim. Shields were often painted in gaudy colours: those found on the Gokstad ship were yellow and black, but written sources also refer to red shields, and to shields brightly painted with images of dragons, gods and heroes. Shields were about 3 ft (1 m) in diameter and covered the

### POPULAR BRAND

Some of the Vikings' finest sword-blades were imported from the Frankish Empire, and many are inlaid with the signature of a German smith named Ulfbehrt – one of the first brand names in European history.

area between chin and thighs. For additional protection, the wealthier warriors might boast a coat of chain mail, known as a byrnie.

Heads were sometimes protected by helmets, and picture-stones depict warriors in conical types with nosepieces. The horned or winged type so often depicted by Victorian book illustrators probably never existed; it was based on a misinterpretation of Nordic images showing horned religious figures. In reality, iron helmets of any kind are so rarely found at Viking sites that scholars believe them to have been the prerogative of higher ranking warriors. Only one complete example, dome-shaped with a central crest and a spectacle-like visor, dating from the 10th century, has survived.

### UNDER THE BANNER OF THE RAVEN

By the second half of the 9th century much had changed compared with the days when small bands of Norse farmer-warriors set out in their boats on opportunistic raids in order to supplement their agricultural income. At the height of Viking power,

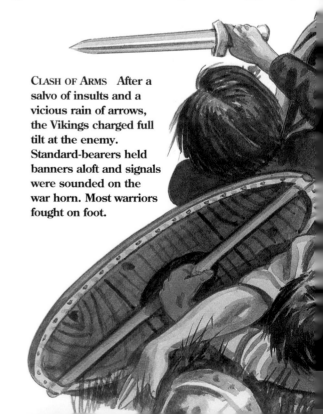

**CLASH OF ARMS  After a salvo of insults and a vicious rain of arrows, the Vikings charged full tilt at the enemy. Standard-bearers held banners aloft and signals were sounded on the war horn. Most warriors fought on foot.**

warriors were organised into sizable armies and fought not only for loot but also for territory and political control. On a long campaign, warriors might be required to spend as much as 30 years away from home – scarcely suitable for a farmer with fields to sow and harvest annually. In the old days, war leaders had recruited agricultural labourers and even household servants, who were obliged to do service on pain of being outlawed. In the age of conquest, the warriors were more likely to be seasoned campaigners and paid mercenaries recruited in the towns and fighting for a share of the loot.

Mobility, surprise and sheer ferocity were always the Norsemen's main assets; strategy and tactics were fairly basic and they were vulnerable when they came up against organised opposition, such as the Moors in Spain. Despite their love of horses the Vikings generally fought on foot, for cavalry was not easily carried in the longships. Horses seized from the enemy might be used for transport and by scouts checking on enemy movements, but written sources strongly suggest that the Vikings lacked significant cavalry forces. In this they differed from the horse-riding Franks with whom they often did battle.

# THE CHOOSERS OF THE SLAIN

FANS OF WAGNERIAN opera know the Valkyries as romantic figures – handmaidens of the war god Odin, they bore dead warriors from the field of battle to the hall of Valhalla, the Viking heaven. And the later Norse myths do represent them in this light. The word 'Valkyrie' means 'chooser of the slain', and the supernatural female beings were supposed to roam battle sites, seeking out the bravest fighters from among the men killed. The dead warriors would be needed by Odin to fight the great battle against the demons on the day of Ragnarok – the end of the world of gods and men.

In earlier myths, however, the Valkyries were more sinister figures: demonic scavengers who feasted like wolves and ravens on the battlefield corpses. In a poem preserved in *Njal's Saga*, the Valkyries wove the web of war on a bloody loom whose warp was of human entrails, while the weft was crimson red. The shuttles were arrows and human heads served as weights:

*It is terrible now*
*To look around,*
*As a blood-red cloud*
*Darkens the sky.*
*The heavens are stained*
*With the blood of men,*
*As the Valkyries*
*Sing their song...*

**HANDMAIDEN**
**This pendant of a female figure, from Sweden, is thought to represent a Valkyrie.**

When the two sides came into conflict, the Vikings would take up a position on terrain inhospitable to horsemen and dig pits against the enemy cavalry.

Before fighting began, the Viking war leader would address his warriors with a rousing speech, and it was also the Norse habit to rattle weapons and hurl insults as an overture to battle. Combat opened with volleys of javelins, arrows and stones raining down on the enemy to soften them up before, with wild battle cries, the warriors charged. The Vikings' shock troops were the *berserkers*, who fought in a frenzy, like wild beasts. The sagas speak of these men as inspired by the god Odin's rage, who 'fought with the madness of dogs or wolves, biting the shield-edge; they had all the strength of bears or bulls. They beat down all opposition, and

**HARD HAT**   **A Viking-Age helmet from Kiev, an area of Scandinavian influence in Russia. The helmet was hammered from sheet iron.**

were themselves neither touched by fire nor iron.'

Signals were sounded on horns, and in pitched battle Viking warriors sometimes organised themselves in a wedge-shaped formation. But most battles must have been confused affairs. The warrior's main point of reference was the standard, indicating where his leader stood. The banner was marked with an emblem such as Odin's raven, and it was the job of a particularly staunch warrior to keep the standard waving aloft and at all cost prevent it from falling into the enemy's hands. This was more than a point of honour; chaos threatened if the standard-bearer failed and the banner vanished into the sea of hacking and thrusting combatants. The king, of course, had the loftiest standard and often fought at the head of the army with a bodyguard of his best warriors around him. Other units, organised in clannish groups of friends and relations, had banners of their own. Superstitious victims of Viking aggression credited the standards with supernatural powers. The Welsh-born monk, Asser, reported: 'They say, moreover, that in every battle, wherever that flag went before them, if they were to gain the victory a live crow would appear flying in the middle of the flag; but if they were doomed to be defeated it would hang down motionless, and this was often proved so.'

To die in battle was considered a glorious thing by the Vikings; honour in death is a recurrent theme in poetry and also on the rune stones carved in memory of the slain. One, commemorating a warrior named Asbjorn, proclaimed that:

> *He fled not*
> *at Uppsala*
> *but struck*
> *while he had weapon.*

Meanwhile, the victors divided up the spoils, which were carried to a pole in the middle of the battlefield and shared out among the warriors according to rank.

### THE SIEGE OF PARIS

The exact size of the Viking forces is unknown. In the later 9th century, when large armies were assembled to invade England, Anglo-Saxon chroniclers referred to fleets of 200 to 300 ships. Since it is reckoned that each vessel carried an average of perhaps 50 warriors, some historians have made fairly low estimates of numbers: a Viking invasion force perhaps amounted to not much more than 1000 men. This might seem inadequate for attempting

**SEABORNE ASSAULT**
**The invasion of Britain by the Danes, as depicted in a 14th-century manuscript.**

the conquest of a nation, which the invaders ultimately intended on this occasion, but it should be remembered that the opposition consisted of badly

---

**EYEWITNESS**

# 'MASSACRE, BURNING AND PLUNDER'

AFTER THE DEATH of Charlemagne in 814 the Frankish Empire went into catastrophic decline. By the middle of the 9th century, Viking marauders were striking deep into France, looting monasteries and torching villages. The unrelenting terror is described by a French monk, Ermentarius, who in 835 fled the monastery of Noirmoutier, at the mouth of the Loire, as a result of Viking attacks:

❛ The number of ships increases, the endless flood of Vikings never ceases to grow. Everywhere Christ's people are the victims of massacre, burning and plunder, clear proof of which will remain as long as the world endures. The Vikings overrun all that lies before them, and none can withstand them. They seize the cities of Bordeaux, Perigueux, Limoges, Angouleme, Toulouse; Angers, Tours and Orleans are made deserts; the ashes of many a saint are carried away. Thus little by little is coming to pass the prophecy spoken by the Lord through the mouth of his prophet (Jeremiah): "Out of the North a scourge shall break forth upon all the inhabitants of the earth."

Ships past counting voyage up the Seine, and throughout the entire region evil grows strong. Rouen is invaded, sacked and set on fire; Paris, Beauvais and Meaux are taken, the fortress of Melun is laid to waste, Chartres occupied, Evreux and Bayeux looted and every town infested. ❜

**MASSED ATTACK**  Danish invaders in England attack a well-fortified and defended town and massacre the inhabitants, from an English manuscript of around 1130.

organised peasant units drawn from the local population. History furnishes more dramatic examples of small trained forces winning out against overwhelming odds: in the 16th century, it took only 500 Spanish conquistadores to subdue the entire Aztec civilisation.

In ferocious assaults the Vikings swept panic-stricken peasant militias from the field of battle, but walled towns presented more of a challenge to their military abilities. In 885, a great army of Norsemen under a leader called Siegfried sailed up the Seine in a fleet estimated by the French priest Abbo of Fleury to have numbered 700 ships carrying 40 000 men. This may be a wild exaggeration, but the fleet was evidently very large by Viking standards.

The aim was to subdue the rich land of Burgundy in eastern France, and to reach it the invaders had to pass the walled city of Paris, which commanded the river from an island connected to the river bank by two fortified bridges. When attempts to negotiate a safe passage failed, the Vikings laid siege to the city. According to Abbo of Fleury: 'The Vikings made three huge siege engines out of immense oak trees which they bound together and mounted in sixteen wheels. A battering ram was rigged up inside each machine and covered by a high roof. They concealed as many as sixty men inside each one. The Vikings finished one, then another and were at work on a third when death came to them from the archers on the walls.'

The siege of Paris proved to be a long drawn-out affair that demonstrated the Vikings' limitations in this kind of warfare. After the initial assault failed, the attackers tried again.'Thousands of lead balls from their slings fell like hail upon the city and powerful catapults were fired at the walls.' Yet

## A PASSION FOR SILVER

The Vikings took astonishing quantities of silver from England, whether as loot or extorted as the protection money known as Danegeld. In Sweden, archaeologists have found more than 30 000 early English coins – more than have turned up in England itself.

ALFRED'S JEWEL
**England's King Alfred, who commissioned this superb ornament, defeated the Vikings in 878.**

Paris withstood the onslaught and the Vikings withdrew for the time being. Early in 886 they tried again, only to meet with even more determined resistance from the defenders, who poured burning oil onto their siege engines. 'Furious at being unable to bring their foe into the open, the Northmen took three ships, filled them with wood and set fire to them. A favourable wind bore the burning vessels towards the bridge but they lodged against its stone piers and burned away harmlessly. The defenders sallied forth and destroyed them.' Storm weather eventually came to the Vikings' aid. It was only when one of the bridges collapsed under pressure from the flood waters of the Seine that Viking ships were able to pass upriver. Other Norsemen continued the siege, but Paris endured all and was eventually relieved by the army of the Frankish emperor, King Charles the Fat.

### CONQUERORS AND COLONISTS

In England, Viking achievements were impressive. From 850, raiders took to wintering on British shores, and in 865 an army encamped on the Isle of Thanet demanding payments of Danegeld – protection money – as the price for leaving the people of Kent in peace. In the same year a 'great heathen army' composed chiefly of Danes invaded East Anglia and moved northwards, capturing York in November 866. The invaders then embarked on a long, zigzag march across the country, setting up winter quarters at a succession of different towns over a 15 year period, crushing resistance and enforcing 'peace agreements' with demands for silver and provisions. In the course of their peregrinations, the Vikings conquered three kingdoms – East Anglia, Mercia and Northumbria.

However, the fourth kingdom, Wessex, under its king, Alfred the Great, managed to hold out against the invaders. This enterprising war leader, forced into hiding in the marshes of Somerset, secretly rallied an army of resistance and went on to triumph against the invaders at the Battle of Edington (878). A monk called Asser reported that, 'fighting fiercely against the whole Viking army, Alfred won the victory. After beating the Vikings, he chased them back to their fortress. Then he boldly made camp in front of their fortress with all his army. Two weeks later, the Vikings, terrified by hunger, cold and fear, asked for peace.' Under the terms of the peace agreement, the Vikings undertook to leave Wessex, and their leader, Guthrum, agreed to be baptised a Christian.

Guthrum was duly baptised (with Alfred acting as godfather), and though the Viking broke the treaty not long afterwards, he made another in 886 that effectively split England into two areas. The south and west became the English kingdom of Wessex; the north and east, under Viking control, became known as the Danelaw because Danish rather than English laws were in force there. Fighting between Saxons and Vikings continued at intervals long afterwards. Between 901 and 937 the English slowly reconquered the Danelaw, but in the reign of Ethelred the Unready (978-1016) the whole of England fell into Danish hands. The longships returned with new demands for the Danegeld, and so great was the terror they inspired that they were able to insist on ever-increasing sums: in 994 they received 16 000 lb (7260 kg) of silver. In 1002 the sum was 24 000 lb (10 890 kg) and in 1007, 36 000 lb (16 330 kg).

Elsewhere in the British Isles the Vikings also put down roots, colonising parts of northern Scotland, the Isle of Man and Ireland. Towns such as Dublin, Cork and Limerick owe their origins to the Norsemen, who founded them as trading stations and bases for seaborne raids. In France, meanwhile, the Vikings settled the rich and fertile farmlands of Normandy. At the beginning of the 10th century the despairing Frankish king, Charles the Simple, offered Rollo, a Norwegian chief, a grant of land in the north of his kingdom if the Norseman would repel other Viking attacks on his beleaguered realm. Rollo agreed – in his own uncouth fashion. According to one account, when the bystanders suggested to the Viking that he ought to kiss the foot of his benefactor, he refused to kneel down but instead grabbed the king's foot and dragged it to his mouth while the monarch was still standing. Losing balance, the king fell to the ground: the Vikings roared with laughter.

Rollo was granted the territory that his men already held, between the Epte and Risle rivers. From this foothold, he and his successors later extended their control to the whole of what is now Normandy. Viking mercenaries from far and wide converged on the region, and in 914 Brittany also fell to the invaders. However, the Norsemen never attempted to subdue the whole Frankish Empire, as they did England. Weak as it had become since the death of Charlemagne, it remained too large and fragmented in its administration for outright conquest to be an option.

### DEFENCE WORKS

When Viking raiders first took to setting up camp on foreign soil, they would often erect a simple fort to serve as a winter base. The practice was long known to scholars through written sources, but only in 1974 did archaeologists identify such a site. In that year, while excavating an Anglo-Saxon church at Repton in Derbyshire, England, investigators made the dramatic discovery of a huge ditch and earthwork rampart. The bank extended from the Church of St Wystan, which the invaders evidently employed as a fortified gateway. The D-shaped fortification backed onto the River Trent and formed an enclosure of about 3³/₄ acres (1.5 ha). Researchers discovered several Viking graves by the church, the most interesting of which belonged to a middle-aged man who had died from a serious wound to the hip. The warrior was laid to rest with his sword and dagger. He also wore a Thor's hammer as a lucky charm around his neck, and was buried with other amulets – a jackdaw's legbone and a wild boar's tusk – in a pouch.

Coins unearthed during the dig date the find to

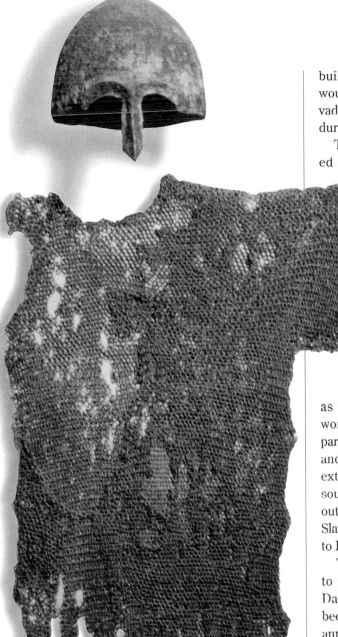

**CHAIN MAIL** A mail shirt of this type would have been worn by Viking warriors to protect themselves from sword blows.

873-4. This was the precise time when, according to the *Anglo-Saxon Chronicle*, the Vikings set up a winter headquarters at Repton, then in the Kingdom of Mercia. The site of Repton Winter Camp has revealed more: a little way outside the defensive ditch was a Saxon mortuary chapel where about 249 Vikings had been buried around the body of their chief. Most were the bones of well built men who seemed not to have died of battle wounds. Scholars believe that members of the invading army must have succumbed to an epidemic during a grim winter at Repton.

The building of defensive works abroad presented no problem to the Vikings. They had gained plenty of practice in Scandinavia, for their own homeland was racked by pirate attacks, dynastic quarrels and boundary disputes that called for forts to be built for communal protection. In Sweden alone, archaeologists have identified almost 1000 hill-forts dating back to the 9th century or earlier.

Viking-Age Denmark was, meanwhile, protected to the south by one of the largest ancient defences in northern Europe. Known as the Danevirke, this great complex of earthworks, consisting of a series of ditches and ramparts that linked in with natural obstacles, was built and added to over many years to form a barrier extending for about 18 miles (30 km) across the southern neck of Jutland. The aim was to screen out hostile neighbours – the Frisians, Franks and Slavs, who all at different times presented a threat to Denmark's security.

The fortification also served, more specifically, to protect the burgeoning town of Hedeby. The Danevirke's original earth and timber rampart has been dated by study of the timbers to 737. Frankish annals report that in 808 Denmark's King Godfred extended it, and archaeology indicates that in 968 a new section was built by Denmark's King Harald Bluetooth.

Harald Bluetooth was also responsible, in around 980, for building a number of imposing royal fortresses across Denmark. Those at Fyrkat in Jutland and Trelleborg on the island of Sjaelland are the most thoroughly excavated, but it is interesting that all share the same strictly geometrical design. The forts had a circular rampart of earth and timber with entrances at the four points of the compass. Ruler-straight streets led in and crossed at the centre so that the circle was divided into four equal segments. Within each quadrant were timber buildings constructed to a standard pattern and laid out around a square. According to one early theory, the fortresses served as barracks and training camps for Vikings destined for the conquest of England. However, research has revealed that, besides warriors, the buildings housed women, children and craftsmen such as blacksmiths and jewellers. It is thought today that the fortresses were likely to have been administrative centres for regional control and tax collection, garrisoned in case of unrest among the local population. They were well positioned to command land routes, although less well placed for coastal duties.

### PUTTING DOWN ROOTS

When the Vikings settled foreign countries, they sent for their wives and children and proceeded to plough the land. Scandinavian place names in Britain betray the areas of Viking influence. One widespread group consists of names ending in -by (indicating a village) as in Whitby, Grimsby and Derby. Others are -thorpe (also a village), -beck (a brook), -holm (a small island) and -thwaite (a clearing). The Viking occupation also left an indelible imprint on everyday speech. Some 600 English words are Norse in origin, among them the nouns knife, egg, husband and window; the adjectives gawky, awkward, ugly and ill; and the verbs to call, to take and to die.

The changes that took place in the lives of ordinary people under the Viking occupation are harder to assess. Within the area of the Danelaw in England, no literature was written; Northumbria's great tradition of monastic writing was extinguished as the Vikings' realm became a graveyard of scholarship. The number of Scandinavians who settled the Danelaw is not known, and by comparison with the multitude of Scandinavian place names that have survived, archaeological finds are relatively few in number. This has suggested to scholars that the Viking immigrants quickly adapted to

## VIKING FORTRESSES

DIFFERENT fortifications were built to serve different needs. The camp at Repton in England was a winter base erected around 873-4 for warriors campaigning on foreign soil. The Vikings took advantage of the site's natural attributes. They evidently saw the defensive potential of the Anglo-Saxon church, sited on its bluff commanding the River Trent. Having occupied the building, they set up bank and ditch defences extending to the cliffs at the water's edge. The church then served them as a fortified gatehouse whose doors offered the only access to the enclosure.

Fyrkat, in the east of Jutland, was different. This was one of several royal fortresses built in the 10th century as an administrative centre and garrison for the soldiery of Denmark's King Harald Bluetooth. The royal forts varied in size, but all followed a virtually identical blueprint. From the circular earth rampart, gateways at the four points of the compass gave access to timber-paved streets that intersected at the centre. Fyrkat's rampart required 353 150 cu ft (10 000 m³) of earth and turf to be shifted, and the outer face was walled for defence with stout tongue-and-grooved timbers.

Inside each of the four quadrants were barrack-like timber buildings arranged to form a hollow square, with a rectangular building in the centre of each square. The 'barrack halls' were boat-shaped, with walls that bowed out and required outer posts to support them at the junction with the curved roof. Several served as living quarters for the inhabitants of the fort, but some were used as workshops and smithies, or as storerooms. The whole has been likened in its perfection to the layout of a Roman legionary camp.

The royal forts bear the stamp of a disciplined workforce and of a degree of centralised state control unknown to the Vikings of earlier centuries.

**ANCIENT DEFENCE** A view of the Danevirke, a massive Viking-Age earthwork constructed to defend the southern frontier of Jutland. Right: The builders extended it over many years.

local English customs – in home-building, manufacturing and burial practices.

Viking York has yielded some of the richest archaeological finds, perhaps because its strong trading connections with the Scandinavian homeland kept the distinctive Norse culture alive. Additional insights have been gained from the *Anglo-Saxon Chronicle*, which refers to a loose confederation of Viking strongholds farther south: Lincoln, Stamford, Leicester, Derby and Nottingham. These Five Boroughs, as they are known, were all well fortified and commanded important routes by land and river in the heart of the country. Inasmuch as the Danelaw had any kind of structured government, it perhaps centred on York and the Five Boroughs.

For local decision-making, the incoming Vikings appear to have held assemblies, or *Things*, as in their homeland. Place names such as Thingoe (Suffolk), Tingewick (Buckingham) and Tingrith (Bedfordshire) all indicate that Things were held there. How local people were treated is a matter for conjecture, but the Vikings' love of liberty and their indepen-

dent spirit evidently survived the immigration. In the Domesday Book, more freemen are referred to in the Danelaw than in other parts of England.

In Normandy, as in England, the Vikings left a wealth of Scandinavian place names but little archaeological evidence of their presence. They seem to have mixed readily with the native people to forge a distinctive Norman identity in which the vigour of the Norsemen was integrated with Frankish culture and Christian faith. Normandy – the land of the Northmen – acquired its present boundaries in 933, and was to launch the last great Viking invasion of England – the Norman Conquest of 1066.

Eirik's wife, Thjodhild, after her conversion to Christianity, which took place along with that of much of the population of Greenland after Olaf Tryggvason, King of Iceland and Norway, sent Eirik's son, Leif, to preach Christianity there.

Buried around the church were 155 people, whose remains have given some insight into the physical condition of the Greenlanders. They were, on the whole, tall and well built. Men measured on average 5 ft 8 in (1.7 m) and several were over 6 ft (1.8 m); the women were 5 ft 3 in (1.6 m). Among both men and women a healthy percentage had reached the age of between 40 and 60.

Brattahlid and the other main centres of development lay in the south of Greenland, but there is clear archaeological evidence that the Vikings also made regular and perilous expeditions to hunting grounds in the far north. Ari the Learned, an Icelandic historian living in the 12th century, reported that they found evidence of human habitation there: remnants of skin boats and stone artefacts. These must have been products of the native Inuit hunter-gatherers – the people formerly known as

Eskimos – whom the Vikings referred to as *skraelings* ('wretches', or 'savages'). Norsemen and Inuit were to have close encounters on the shores of North America, in the course of the greatest Viking adventure of all.

### VIKING AMERICA

'Island-hopping' had brought the Vikings across the Atlantic, from the Faeroes to Iceland, and then to Greenland. One last leap would take them to an entirely new continent whose immensity they perhaps never guessed. A chance sighting of America was made in about 985 by a merchant called Bjarni. He had set sail from Iceland with a valuable cargo to join his parents in Greenland, but was blown off course and sailed on westwards into uncharted waters. According to the sagas, as land was lost to sight below the horizon, 'the fair wind failed and northerly winds and fog set in, and for many days they had no idea what their course was. After that they saw the sun again and were able to get their bearings; they hoisted

**EIRIK'S HOME** Brattahlid, heart of the Eastern Settlement on Greenland, was founded by Eirik the Red. Inset right: A medieval manuscript from the *Hauksbok* tells Eirik's saga.

**AMERICAN OUTPOST** Some Viking buildings at L'Anse aux Meadows, Newfoundland, have been reconstructed. Right: A Norse ringed pin that was found at the site.

sail and after a day's sailing they sighted land. They discussed among themselves what country this might be. Bjarni said that he thought it could not be Greenland.'

The land was well wooded, with low hills. Bjarni did not, however, make any attempt to explore it, but set his prow back towards the north-east for Greenland and his father's home. Credit for the true discovery of America is given to Leif the Lucky, son of Eirik the Red. Some 10 to 15 years after Bjarni's voyage, Leif set out to retrace the merchant's route. Rather than leaving from Iceland, however, he set out from Disko Island, off the Greenland coast, with a crew of 35, and crossed the Davis Strait to reach a rocky and barren land, which he dubbed *Helluland* (Slab Land).

From this stony waste – probably Baffin Island – Leif the Lucky sailed south to another, more agreeable country. 'Once again they sailed right up to it and cast anchor, lowered a boat and went ashore. This country was flat and wooded, with white sandy beaches wherever they went; and the land sloped gently down to the sea.' This second land, which Leif named *Markland* (Forest Land), is thought to have been the coast of Labrador.

Two further days' sailing brought the explorers

to a promontory with an offshore island, where 'They went ashore and looked about them. The weather was fine. There was dew on the grass, and the first thing they did was to get some of it on their hands and put it to their lips, and to them it seemed the sweetest thing they had ever tasted.' This bountiful country Leif called *Vinland* (Vineland) after the wild grapes that his men found growing in the interior. There has been much discussion about this key detail. Vinland is generally identified with Newfoundland, where a site of indisputable Norse origin has been excavated at L'Anse aux Meadows. But even in the milder climate of the 10th and 11th centuries, it is unlikely that grapes flourished at this latitude. Were the wild fruits really grapes, or merely berries (from which the Scandinavians did sometimes ferment drink)? Was L'Anse aux Meadows the site of Vinland itself, or the gateway to a larger settlement farther south?

Wherever the precise location, it is reported that the explorers landed and spent the winter in Vinland before returning home. And the adventure did not end there. According to the sagas, the Norsemen were to return and attempt to found colonies in the New World; they also traded and did battle with the Native Americans.

Stories of the Vikings' American adventure are told – with some inconsistencies – in the *Greenlander Saga* and the *Saga of Eirik the Red*, while stray references crop up in other sources too. For example, in about 1075, long before the saga-writers produced their narratives, the German churchman, Adam of Bremen wrote of an island in the Atlantic: 'It is called Vinland because vines producing excellent wine grow wild there; moreover, self-sown wheat grows there in abundance. It is not from any fabulous imaginings that we have learned this, but from the reliable reports of the Danes.'

In the sagas it is reported that Leif the Lucky encouraged further expeditions after his pioneering trip to Vinland. The year after the first voyage, his brother Thorwald took a party across to the New World and was killed by an arrow in a clash with the Native Americans. Subsequently, an Icelander named Thorfinn Karlsefni made a determined effort to colonise Vinland, founding a settlement of perhaps 160 people and 'all kinds of livestock'. It

failed, however, after only three years, due to ever worsening relations with the native peoples.

Who were these indigenous people? The sagas describe them in derogatory terms as dark-skinned, ugly folk with coarse, untidy hair, large eyes and broad cheekbones. Their weapons were of stone, they brandished rattle-sticks and travelled in skin-boats. Were these kayaks or canoes? From the passing references in the sagas it is impossible to determine whether the locals were Inuit or Native Americans, though some scholars incline to the view that they were probably the latter – Stone Age ancestors of the Native American Montagnais tribe. It seems that at first they traded with the Norsemen, exchanging furs and pelts for the colonists' milk and red cloth. But things deteriorated when the native peoples realised that they were being exploited. Fighting broke out and the Norsemen were outnumbered by the local inhabitants. The colonists' supply lines with Greenland were, moreover, hopelessly overstretched and easily cut by bad weather. In the end, the Vikings packed up and went home.

## EYEWITNESS

# VIKINGS AND INDIANS

IN THE *SAGA OF EIRIK THE RED*, first recorded in a medieval manuscript, a party of Norse settlers, including Eirik's daughter Freydis, in the Vinland colony in North America is attacked one spring by Native Americans – whom the Vikings referred to as *skraelings* ('wretches') – the two groups having previously traded peacefully:

● They saw a large number of canoes paddling towards them once more. The flails (rattle-sticks) were waved in each boat and Karlsefni and his men raised their shields and they traded together. Most of the skraelings wanted to buy red

cloth and offered furs and skins in return. They also wanted swords but Karlsefni would not allow his men to sell them.

Next moment, the bull belonging to Karlsefni and his men rushed out of the forest bellowing loudly. The skraelings were so terrified that they raced back to their canoes and paddled away. Nothing more was heard of them for three weeks. Then, a great fleet of canoes came up the river from the south. This time the flails were waved about in a different way and all the skraelings were yelling so fiercely that Karlsefni and his men took out

their red shields. The skraelings leapt from their canoes, charged at the Vikings and they fought together. There was a heavy shower of stones, as the skraelings had slings. Karlsefni and his men saw the skraelings hoisting a large blue-black ball up a pole which made a hideous noise when they released it. The Vikings were terrified and ran away hoping to escape along the river. They ran until they reached some rocks where they defended themselves bravely. They were saved by a woman called Freydis who seized a sword and frightened the skraelings away. ●

# How Did the Vikings Navigate?

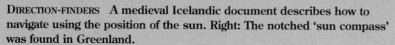

**DIRECTION-FINDERS** A medieval Icelandic document describes how to navigate using the position of the sun. Right: The notched 'sun compass' was found in Greenland.

NORSE SEAMEN had no maps or magnetic compasses for finding their way at sea. Yet they managed to cross vast tracts of ocean out of sight of land. How did they navigate?

Some directions were probably estimated relative to the sun and the stars. The Pole Star, in particular, may have helped in gauging latitude: the farther north the seamen travelled, the higher the Pole Star appeared in the sky. Norse mariners also came to recognise wind directions and sea currents.

Evidence of land beyond the horizon could be discerned by interpreting cloud patterns, the behaviour of sea birds, or the sudden appearance of twigs and branches in the sea.

A Viking explorer called Floki is said to have taken ravens with him on one of his trips, and released them so that in flying high above the ship they would see farther than the crewmen on deck. When one freed bird returned to the ship, Floki knew there could be no land in sight. A second bird also returned. When a third flew off beyond the horizon, Floki followed – and discovered Iceland.

The mariner's magnetic compass was not introduced until the 12th century – after the end of the Norse era. But it is thought that Arab navigators of the 9th and 10th centuries may have employed a simple wooden measuring device, called a *kamal*, to calculate the height of the Pole Star. The Vikings were in contact with the Arabs and may have learnt of the instrument from them.

It has also been suggested that the Vikings used a simple sun compass to make estimates of direction. The evidence derives from part of a wooden disc excavated by Danish archaeologist C.L. Vebaek from a Norse site in eastern Greenland. It was cut from spruce or larch and has been dated to around AD 1000. Notches around the edge appear to mark the points of a compass, while incised lines on the surface may correspond to the sun's path at the equinoxes and the summer solstice. Scholars believe that the shadows cast by a central gnomon, a wooden cone like that of a sundial, may have assisted in taking bearings.

# TOWNS AND TRADES

The bustling wharves of Scandinavian seaports bore witness to the Vikings' commercial flare. Norse traders took furs, slaves, walrus tusks and amber to the hot shores of the Mediterranean.

Silks and spices reached their homeland from the exotic East.

THE SAVAGE romance of the Vikings' reputation as pirates and sea warriors tends to obscure their achievements in trade and commerce. Dominance of north European seas and rivers allowed Norse merchants to open up trade routes over long distances and develop sizable markets and trading towns. The amount of plundered silver in circulation also contributed. Foreign merchants flocked to Scandinavia's urban centres: Saxons, Frisians, Slavs and Arabs among them.

It is not hard to picture the excitement of local people crowding the wharves of a Viking trading port to see what luxuries the latest merchant ship would bring in. Wine, glassware and weapons arrived from the European heartland; silks, spices and jewellery came from Byzantium and the exotic East. Trade links extended over remarkably long distances. One of the most astonishing finds ever made at a pre-Viking

**EXOTIC CHARM**
**A bronze Buddha from Helgö in Sweden.**

site was the discovery at Helgö, Sweden, of a bronze Buddha from north India. The statuette, which shows the Enlightened One sitting on a lotus throne, seems to have been worn as an amulet by its owner, for it had a leather thong tied around it when found. Precisely how it reached Helgo will never be known; it may have been passed from hand to hand through trade or – conceivably – brought back from the East by a single traveller.

**'ALL HEDEBY WAS BLAZING'**
To pay for their imports the Vikings exported a wealth of commodities of their own. Slaves and furs from the far north were highly prized as far south as the Mediterranean. The Vikings also exported timber, salt fish, honey, walrus tusks, sealskins, feathers and down, iron ore, tar, whetstones (for sharpening knives), and amber from the Baltic Sea. Soapstone was among

continued on page 104

## EYEWITNESS

# 'AT THE END OF THE WORLD OCEAN'

THE GREAT Viking port of Hedeby failed to impress an Arab visitor, Al-Tartushi, travelling in Scandinavia in the 10th century. A merchant from Cordoba, he was familiar with the much more sophisticated cities of the Mediterranean and referred to Hedeby as a 'town at the very end of the world ocean', although some of his claims may be exaggerated:

❛ They hold a festival where they assemble to honour their god and eat and drink. Anyone who slaughters an animal by way of sacrifice has a pole outside his house door and hangs the sacrificed animal there, whether it be an ox or ram, he-goat or boar, so that people may know that he makes sacrifice in honour of his god. The town is

poorly off for goods and wealth. The people's chief food is fish, for there is so much of it. If a child is born there it is thrown into the sea to save bringing it up... I have never heard more horrible singing than the slesvigers' – it is like a growl coming out of their throats, like the barking of dogs, only much more beastly. ❜

# VIKING CRAFTSMEN

TOILING IN THE workshops that line a town street, specialist craftsmen shape some of the wares needed in everyday Viking life. In the foreground, a carpenter makes bowls on a lathe, which he operates by treadle. In the booth beyond, an antler-carver fashions a comb. Across the street iron bars scatter the ground at a forge, where a weaponsmith shapes a blade. Down the street, women weave cloth on an upright loom. People often worked in the open air, where lighting and ventilation were better than indoors. Goods were not only for home consumption: overseas trade flourished due to both seaward expansion and silver, which gave the Scandinavians purchasing power.

**AMBER HEADS** Pieces of amber, washed up on Baltic beaches, provided a valuable raw material for trading with the Mediterranean lands.

the Vikings' most distinctive exports: it was quarried in Norway and shipped in roughly shaped blocks to other foreign centres, where it would be shaped to make household vessels.

Thus trade helped to foster industry. Ports such as Birka in Sweden and Hedeby in Denmark began to flourish as manufacturing centres that turned out a range of craft products: bronze jewellery, amber pendants, deer-antler combs and leather footwear, for sale both at home and abroad. Some trades were very specialised; at Birka archaeologists have uncovered the workshops of craftsmen who prepared fox and squirrel skins for use in trimming garments. Ribe in Denmark was a centre for the mass production of glass beads: fragments of broken glass imported from the Rhineland were melted down and rolled in small lumps on an iron rod to form tiny cylindrical or spherical beads.

Among many important sites, Hedeby is the most thoroughly investigated settlement of the Viking Age. Tucked into the eastern side of Jutland, this was the most southerly town in Scandinavia and ideally placed to be a crossroads for trade with the rest of Europe. The earliest layers of settlement date from the 8th century, and it is clear that by the 10th century it was a bustling urban centre, surrounded by a rampart that linked it to the defensive wall across southern Jutland known as the Danevirke.

Some of Hedeby's houses were built of planks, but most were of wattle and daub, while the poor lived at one end of town in damp, sunken pits covered with thatched roofs. The site must have been muddy: the stream running through the settlement had planked sides to stop it flooding its banks, and the streets were wood-planked, too. But the sodden ground notwithstanding, Hedeby flourished and

merchants travelled long distances to reach it. Among the 340 000 objects found there are artefacts from as far away as Baghdad. Hedeby was visited in about 950 by an Arab merchant, Al-Tartushi, who left an oft-quoted account of the town, and it is also mentioned in other foreign written sources.

Because of its wealth Hedeby was a target for attack, and at various times the town was in Danish, German and Swedish possession. Often besieged and often plundered, it was burned to the ground in 1049 by the Norwegian King Harald Hardrada. Layers of sooty earth at the site testify to the calamity, which was celebrated by a Norwegian minstrel who gloated over the humiliation of Denmark's King Svein Estridson:

> *All Hedeby was blazing,*
> *Fired by Harald's fury;*
> *There's no limit to the boldness of Norway's*
> *warrior sea-king.*
> *King Svein now feels the havoc*
> *Of Harald's deadly vengeance.*
> *At dawn on Hedeby's outskirts*
> *I saw the tall fires raging.*

### VIKING YORK

While commerce transformed the Norse homeland, it also stimulated town-building abroad. The Vikings set up trading posts wherever they sailed. Before the Norsemen arrived, Ireland, for example, had been a village society, lacking any significant trade contacts with the outside world. Under Viking influence, commercial ports began to spring up all around the coast of

**IMPORTS** These glass gaming pieces, possibly Egyptian, were found in Sweden.

**MEDIEVAL SPIRES** The earliest known representation of York, known to the Vikings as Jorvik. The city was their main power base in England. Right: A Norse craftsman's sharpening stone from Jorvik.

Ireland. The country's first towns – Dublin, Limerick, Waterford and Wicklow – were all Scandinavian in origin.

The biggest trading centre in England was York, known in Old Norse as Jorvik. Founded originally by the Romans, the town was captured by a great Viking army on All Saints' Day (November 1) in 866. Shortly afterwards, Norse settlers moved in to set up homes and workshops, and the town grew to become the main focus of Scandinavian power on English soil. An English monk wrote of it around 1000 as 'a city made rich by the wealth of merchants who come from everywhere, but especially from the Danish people'. It is estimated that by 1066 York had over 10 000 inhabitants.

In 1976 a factory was knocked down on a street called Coppergate in York, and archaeologists were able to investigate the site and reveal the vestiges of dwellings and workshops that lay below. The name Coppergate came from the Old Norse *koppr*, meaning cup. It is evident that people who lived in the street were woodturners, making cups, bowls and plates in the yards behind their houses.

Other craftworkers in York included jewellers, metalsmiths and shoemakers. The remains of a coin mint was found, and there was a workshop that specialised in making combs out of antler and bone. The excavated tenement plots stretched from their street frontage back towards the wharves on the Fosse. All were about 18 ft (5.5 m) wide, which might suggest planning by a central authority. However, it could be that experience had taught that this was the optimum area that allowed the needs of reasonable comfort to be balanced with the need to cram the maximum number of properties into a town street.

Conditions indoors were squalid. The buildings' floors were of bare earth whose level rose as, day by day, the occupants carried in mud on the soles of their shoes. Bits of household rubbish and craftworkers' debris were simply discarded on the floors and trampled in. Outside, too, the ground level rose with the accumulation of mud and rotting vegetation. In the yard, the cesspit and rubbish heap lay hard by the storage pit and water

105

**VIKING TOOLKIT   Assorted implements found in Viking York. Excavations in the city have revealed the presence of woodturners, leatherworkers, antler-comb makers, metalsmiths and coin-makers.**

well. Burial practices were scarcely hygienic; evidence has been found of the haphazard disposal of corpses in impromptu pits. These may have been the victims of street brawls or battles. The *Anglo-Saxon Chronicle* reports that in 867, the year after the Vikings seized York, the Angles gathered a large army and attacked the city: 'Some of them got inside, and an immense slaughter was made of them, some inside and some outside.'

Research at York has shown that the population was infested with fleas, lice and intestinal worms. And with such unhealthy living conditions it is scarcely surprising that life expectancy was low. Over a quarter of York's inhabitants died in childhood; over half the women died before they reached 35; and only one person in ten lived to 60. Yet such statistics were not exceptional for towns of the era, and amid all its squalor York continued to thrive as a royal centre that distributed luxury goods from all over the known world.

York was in Viking hands until 954, when the last Scandinavian king was ousted. During the years of Norse control its lively wharves received German wine and pottery; Norwegian soapstone; brooches from the Low Countries; dress pins from Ireland; and Byzantine silks. In one building at York archaeologists discovered a small decorative cowrie shell of the species *Cypraea pantherina*. This exists only in the Red Sea and the Gulf of Aden, demonstrating just how far flung the town's contacts were.

### DOWN THE DNIEPER

Adventures as fantastic in their way as the settlement of Greenland and North America were undertaken by the Viking traders who headed east and south, nosing down long rivers deep into the interior of Europe and Russia. The great waterways of the Danube, Vistula, Dnieper and Volga provided ready-made arteries for the Norse explorers and merchants, who moved freely through the Slavic lands, setting up trading posts where they went. Some, travelling on via the Black Sea and the Caspian Sea, reached fabled Constantinople (Istanbul), capital of the Byzantine Empire (also known as the Eastern Roman Empire), and even Baghdad, residence of the Arab caliphs.

Here were vast resources of gold, silver and other

## REFUSE DISPOSAL

Rubbish accumulated continuously on the floors of Viking town houses. In 10th-century York, the ground level rose at an average rate of 1in (2 cm) every year.

coveted treasures. A huge influx of Arab silver, in particular, reached the Viking homeland between about 800 and 1015 – some presumably from the Caliphate, but much also circulating in Russia, where it helped to stimulate the expanding trade network. There were important Arab silver mines in the Samanid area of central Asia, and the coins themselves were often struck at Samarkand and Tashkent. In exchange, the Vikings offered furs, slaves, walrus ivory, honey, wax and amber. Russia was the great trading ground. Many Viking graves have been excavated in her riverside towns, and judging by the fact that the Norsemen were often buried in cemeteries among the local inhabitants it appears that relations were friendly. The Scandinavians certainly put down roots in Russia, but their settlements always clung to the banks of the rivers.

They did, however, go raiding for slaves in the countryside around, and it is likely that they plundered silver from these people; silver was also extorted from local people as protection money. The river journeys were themselves fraught with such dangers as cataracts, rapids and swirling currents. A Byzantine document describes how traders would try to negotiate a course between the jagged rocks, sometimes stripping naked to leap into the water and feel the way with their bare feet, using poles to steady the boat. In some impassable places, the ships had to be dragged overland to reach another river. When facing such hazards, the Vikings were particularly vulnerable to attack by hostile local tribes. In Sweden, many rune stones dating from the 11th century record these perilous expeditions; one commemorates a Swedish trader who died in the Dnieper's rapids.

### THE LAND OF THE RUS

While the Scandinavians who crossed the Atlantic were mostly Norwegians and Danes, those who went south and east were chiefly Swedish Vikings. Of some 85 000 Arab coins that have been found by

# READING THE RUNES

**SIGN LANGUAGE** An incised stone from Sweden displays the earlier, 24 rune alphabet.

RUNIC INSCRIPTIONS have been found on a wealth of objects, from solemn commemorative stones to the odd piece of bone with nothing more portentous than the message 'Kiss me' incised upon it. Viking runes were specially well suited to cutting in wood, and wooden sticks were often carved for everyday purposes such as messages, bills and accounts. The characters were carved chiefly in straight lines, rather than hard-to-cut curves, and were mainly made up of verticals and diagonals. Presumably, the grain of the wood made horizontal lines more awkward to cut.

The runic alphabet is known as the *futhark*, after its first six characters. There were two main variants: the normal alphabet and the so-called 'short-twig runes', which were quicker to carve and useful for day-to-day messages. However, regional differences may also account for the development of two separate alphabets. The normal alphabet was more widespread in Denmark, the short-twig runes in Norway and Sweden and their colonies.

Runes were not an invention of the Vikings. Their alphabet derived from an older script used by several Germanic tribes, which perhaps originated in Greek or Roman models. Primitive writing skills were fairly widespread among the tribes of Iron-Age Europe. The Celts, for example, had an alphabet, and early runes are found in England and the Low Countries.

The Scandinavians were themselves carving runic inscriptions as early as AD 200, long before the Viking Age, and their alphabet possessed 24 characters at that time. The alphabet that had evolved by the Norse era was shorter, however, incorporating only 16 characters. It was not very efficient: there was no symbol for the common vowel *e*, for example, or for the consonants *d*, *g* or *þ*. Other letters approximating to these sounds were used instead, so that, with various inconsistencies in the way that characters were carved, runic messages are often hard to decipher.

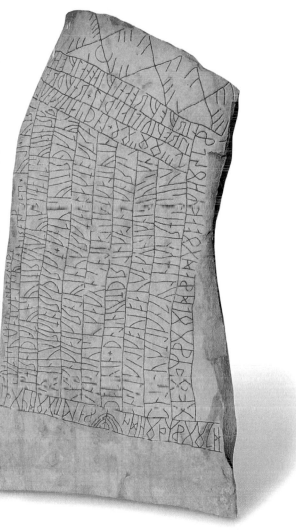

**MIGHTY MONUMENT** Sweden's 7 ft (2 m) Rok Stone bears the longest known runic inscription.

full, too, of strange references and as yet undeciphered symbols that are thought by some scholars to be magic formulas.

The meanings of many of the runic messages, however, were often quite commonplace. For example, they could denote nothing more than simple ownership of property. A weapon found in Ireland bears the text 'Dufnall Sealshead owns this sword'; a casket found in Norway is inscribed, 'Rannveig owns this box'. Other scraps of writing have been found that

**RUNE-CUTTING** The symbols were carved on both rock faces and freestanding boulders.

offer more intriguing glimpses into everyday life. At Maeshowe in the Orkneys, for example, is a Neolithic burial chamber that bears the appealing inscription, 'Ingigero is the sweetest woman there is' – the ancient chamber seems to have been often used by courting couples, who wrote other love graffiti within.

Runic inscriptions, with their enigmatic symbols, were full of mystery for those Vikings who did not understand their meaning. And though most messages were purely functional, people clearly believed that they had occult powers. To those without the knowledge, mastery of the runes implied mastery of strange forces that could be employed either for good or for evil. Standing stones at Blekinge in Sweden invoke a curse on anyone who damages the monument. Runes were carved to cast healing spells, to protect warriors in battle, to guard against witchcraft or to bring bad luck on an enemy. 'May Thor hallow these runes', was a common endpiece to inscriptions from the pagan age.

Rune stones were decorated with elaborate patterns and coloured paint: black, red, blue and white, and sometimes the letters themselves were also painted. The great rune masters considered themselves practitioners of a refined art, and inept rune-carving could, it was thought, do more harm than good.

*Egil's Saga* tells of a woman called Helga who lies ill for night after night upon a bed in her father's longhouse. Egil is told that healing runes were carved for her by a local farmer's son but that she only became worse as a result. Asked if he can help, the hero searches her bed and finds

**GROTESQUE FACE** This image appears on a Danish rune stone commemorating a man named Ful, who died 'when kings fought'.

ten runes crudely carved on whalebone. Egil scratches out the message, burns the piece of whalebone and has the bedclothes removed from the house because they had been contaminated by the badly carved runes. Then he replaces the spell with runes of his own, which he places under the pillow – she soon begins to get better.

### OF KINGS AND OUTLAWS

By contrast with the fragmentary, sometimes inscrutable, nature of the runes, the Norse sagas present an immense pageant of people and events, vibrant with colour and rich in human interest. Here are battles, murders and blood feuds, tales of kings and outlaws, chronicles of historical events such as the struggle to unite Norway under one crown, the settlement of Iceland and Greenland, and the discovery of America. There is no lack of information in the sagas. The problem for the historian lies in sifting the historical fact from the storytellers' fiction.

The sagas were written in Iceland mainly between about 1200 and 1400 – long after the 10th and 11th-century events that they describe. Ranked among the masterpieces of medieval European literature, they cannot be taken too literally as historical truth but are better thought of as historical novels. The sagas contain serious chronological discrepancies and every detail – from law, religion and farming practices to styles of weaponry

---

## EYEWITNESS

# 'HOWLING I LEARNT THEM'

ALTHOUGH RUNES were carved primarily for practical purposes, they were widely believed to be charged with magical significance. This is evident from a passage in the Norse poem *Havamal*, which describes the ordeal undergone by the god Odin, who hung from the World Tree in order to gain secret knowledge of the occult meaning of the runes:

*I know that I hung
On the windswept tree
For nine whole nights,
Pierced by the spear
And given to Odin,
Myself given to myself
On that tree*

*Whose roots
No man knows.
They refreshed me neither with
    bread
Nor with drink from the horn.
I peered down,
I learnt runes,
Howling I learnt them,
And then fell back.*

CUTTING LOOSE  An Icelandic saga illustration shows Norway's King Harald Finehair severing the bonds of his guardian spirit, the giant Dofri.

and dress – has to be treated cautiously for it may reflect a medieval reality rather than a truth about the Viking Age.

Nonetheless, however much scholarly scepticism is applied to the sagas, they cannot be wholly dismissed for they do incorporate a lot of information that is supported by archaeological evidence. The Vinland of the sagas, we now know, was no invention of a medieval fantasist. And many details of everyday life are also confirmed by archaeology. The horse fights described in Icelandic literature, for example, are also depicted on ancient carved stones.

Sometimes, documentary evidence corroborates the saga-writer. For example, *Egil's Saga* describes a man named Thorolf who exacts tributes from the Lapps in skins and furs. The account is matched in many of its details by the 9th-century

## A WEEKLY DIP

It seems that Saturday night was bath night in Viking times. In the Scandinavian languages, the word for Saturday derives from the Old Norse *laugardagur*, meaning 'hot-springs day'.

119

report of the Norwegian seaman, Ottar, who brings Lapp tributes to King Alfred.

Written on vellum (calfskin) with the quills of swans or ravens and ink distilled from berries, the sagas were immensely popular in medieval Iceland, both as entertainment and for the ancestral memories they enshrined. The most interesting to historians fall into two categories of prose narrative: the *Kings' Sagas* and the *Sagas of the Icelanders.* Wholly legendary tales of early Scandinavian rulers serve as an overture to the *Kings' Sagas,* which then proceeds with a life of Harald Finehair, the first king of all Norway. Ruthless and resourceful, he managed through warfare and a series of cunning alliances to unite a scattering of bickering kingdoms into a single political realm, and many people were reported to have left Norway for Iceland in order to avoid his rule.

Harald was a real enough historical character who ruled from about 870 to 940, and the saga follows the dynastic struggles of his successors on the throne of Norway into the Middle Ages. Conflict with the Norwegian Crown in medieval times – and Iceland's attempts to stay independent –

**HOME GUARD** This panel from a carved whalebone casket shows the saga hero Egil as an archer defending his home. Violent and avaricious, Egil was also admired as a bold warrior and gifted poet.

made the theme especially interesting to contemporary readers, and there is a strong focus in the tales on the doings of Icelanders at the Norwegian court.

### TALES OF THE ICELANDERS

The other great body of works are the *Sagas of the Icelanders,* which tell of the settlement of Iceland by the pioneers and their descendants: the masterly *Egil's Saga, Njal's Saga* and *Laxdaela Saga* are among them. Centring as they do on family relationships, with their feuds and alliances, they are often known as the *Family Sagas,* and the tales had an important functional role. Medieval Icelanders wanted to know how much land was claimed by the first settlers and their descendants, for land claims in their own day related back to the pioneers.

The sagas also taught much about the landscape

he grew to be an excellent craftsman.' This is a typical piece of pen-portraiture: an unpleasant man may very well be a good worker, and the author makes no attempt to iron out the contradictions.

The saga-writers were men of learning. Their tone was cool and impartial and they presented events with remarkable objectivity, even when writing about paganism. Although they were Christian scholars, they expressed no ill-feeling towards the ancestral faith of Odin and Thor. In fact, the author of the *Laxdaela Saga* makes a point of instructing his readers: 'Pagans felt their responsibilities no less keenly when performing such ceremonies than Christians do now when ordeals are decreed.'

### A GENIUS FOR POETRY

Few of the saga-writers' names are known today, but one that has survived is that of Snorri Sturluson (1178-1241), author of the *Heimskringla* – the *Circle of the World* – which ranks supreme among the *Kings' Sagas*. A nobleman deeply embroiled in Icelandic politics, Snorri was also a great scholar and quite aware of his duty, as a historian, to quote his sources. He wrote that he obtained some material for his sagas from the historical writings of another scholar, Ari the Learned, who in turn got his own information from 'old intelligent persons'.

Ari, it appears, was a wise and inquisitive man blessed with an excellent memory. Yet Snorri wrote that an even better source was the *skalds*, or Scandinavian poets. The Vikings loved poetry and at feasts both men and women took turns at reciting verse, sometimes making it up as they went along. Because the great hall was often riotous

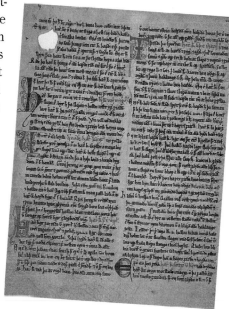

**KING'S STORY** A page from a 14th-century manuscript tells the saga of King Harald Finehair.

itself and how certain places acquired their names. In the *Laxdaela Saga*, for example, a shipwreck is described: 'Throughout the day they saw an enormous seal swimming in the current; it circled the boat all day. It had huge flippers, and everyone thought its eyes were those of a human. Thorstein told his men to harpoon the seal, but all their attempts failed. Then the tide began to rise; but just as the boat was about to be refloated, a violent gust of wind broke upon them and the boat heeled over. Everyone on board was drowned, except for one man called Gudmund who was washed ashore with some timber at a place which has been known as the Gudmundar Isles ever since.'

The stories' appeal always rested above all on their ability to excite and entertain. And part of their interest for the modern reader lies in their portrayals of men and women torn between conflicting loyalties or conflicting character traits – the personalities have human complexities. Yet the style of writing is plain and unadorned. 'Grim was a dark and ugly man, like his father both in appearance and disposition. He became a very efficient man, he was clever with wood and iron, and

with noise, it was common to open a poem with a call for silence. There then followed a series of verses outlining the virtues of the chief who was being addressed. Professional skalds were hired by kings and chieftains to sing their praises, which might make their verses seem dubious historical evidence. However, flattery could only be taken so

THE ENTERTAINER A skald, or poet, regales his audience. The Vikings knew the power of the spoken word. Valued as entertainers, skalds were also feared for their savagely satirical or insulting verses.

## POETRY MAID

Not all of the Viking *skalds* – the professional poets who wrote the complex verse forms that appeared both as occasional poems and in the sagas – were men. The name has survived of one female skald who was active in Norway around 930. Her name was Jorunn Skaldmaer – Jorunn Poetry Maid.

far in the courts of hard-bitten Viking rulers. A poet might exaggerate the valour of a king in describing a famous victory, but he would hardly celebrate a defeat as if it were a triumph. As Ari wrote: 'No one would dare to relate to a chief what he, and all who heard it, knew to be false and imaginary, not a true account of his deeds; because that would be mockery, not praise.'

Moreover, skalds were independent artists rather than paid members of the royal staff. Being unattached to court they were less reliant on the monarch than other courtiers and so could be persuaded to tell the king home truths on occasion. This was the case with a certain Sigvat Thordarson, an 11th-century poet who once gave Norway's King Magnus a dressing-down. The ruler had incurred odium by taking vengeance against the opponents of his father, and a party at court persuaded Sigvat to speak out. The result was a poem called *The Plain-speaking Verses,* in which Sigvat itemised the qualities required of a wise ruler, and warned Magnus of the perils he faced if he persisted in his actions.

So, when all the obvious allowances are made for poetic licence, skaldic verse provides a rich storehouse for the historian. The poems were passed on from generation to generation before being committed to writing towards the end of the 12th century, and their rhythms and rhymes must have made it easier to remember information. Most skaldic poems survive through the

# THE LEGEND OF SIEGFRIED

THE *Ring of the Nibelungen*, the great operatic cycle composed by Richard Wagner (1813-83), dramatises a series of myths that were often told around the hearth in Viking longhouses, though the tales were current among Germanic tribes, too.

The most famous story is that of Siegfried, or Sigurd in the Scandinavian tradition. Norse myths tell how he is the son of a king in the land of the Franks and wins fame and riches by slaying the dragon Fafnir, guardian of a great treasure. Sigurd hides in a pit to achieve his end and stabs the dragon from below with a sword forged from his father's weapon. He then cooks Fafnir's heart, and gets some dragon blood on a finger, which he puts in his mouth. By tasting dragon's blood he learns the language of birds, whose twitterings reveal that the smith Regin, who has forged his sword, intends to betray him and steal the treasure. Sigurd kills the smith and wins the gold. Unknown to the hero, however, the treasure carries a curse with it.

Wealthy and famous, Sigurd exchanges vows of love with Brynhild, one of the Valkyres who select warriors slain in battle to go to heaven. But he is later persuaded through a magic potion to forget his betrothed and fall instead for Gudrun, sister of a Burgundian king. They marry, and Sigurd obtains for her – by deception – the ring he had earlier given to Brynhild. When the Valkyrie finds out, she becomes enraged and connives at Sigurd's death. The hero is stabbed as he lies in bed, and dies in his waking wife's arms. Brynhild then kills herself, asking to be burned on a funeral pyre beside Sigurd. The treasure, still lustrous and still cursed, passes to Gudrun's brothers, Gunnar and Hogni.

**TASTE OF KNOWLEDGE** Sigurd licks the dragon's blood from his finger.

sagas, which, though written in prose, incorporate many stanzas in verse to illuminate the storylines.

Apart from its value to the historian, skaldic verse also exhibits a Norse genius for poetic imagery. The skalds crowded their stanzas with inventive expressions to describe commonplace things. The sea, for example, becomes the 'whale road' or the 'plain of seals'; the warrior is 'the feeder of the raven'; the axe is 'the wood-griever'; a battle is a 'game of iron'; blood is the 'sweat of the sword'. These expressions, known as kennings, so pack skaldic poetry that the text is sometimes very hard to understand. Whole verses read like riddles, designed to delight the initiated – and no doubt confound the dull-witted – with their often bizarre circumlocutions. It may be possible for an imaginative reader to work out that a 'wagon of thought' means a head; a 'speech servant' is a tongue; a 'forehead moon' is an eye. But what is 'Thor's weighty wrestling friend'? The kenning makes sense only to a reader familiar with Norse mythology, for it refers to a tale in which the god Thor challenged his enemies to a wrestling match and did combat with an aged woman who turned out to be Old Age herself. The story had a moral: that senility brings even the mightiest to their knees. 'Thor's weighty wrestling friend', then, means old age.

## NORWEGIAN NURSERY RHYME

The nursery rhyme 'London Bridge is falling down,' is said by some scholars to date back to the time of the Norwegian Viking Olaf Haraldsson. A future king of Norway, he was in his youth a mercenary raider who once pulled down London Bridge, at that time constructed of timber, with grappling irons.

# PAGAN BELIEF

Visions of the demonic god Loki, of the wolf Fenrir and the monstrous World Serpent haunted the

Norse realms of the spirit, along with images of evil giants, cunning dwarfs and fate-weaving

goddesses. Sinister forces threatened even mighty Thor and Odin, the All-Father.

HEAVEN BOUND   A stone carving shows slain warriors on their way to join Odin's elite in Valhalla.

SKALDIC POETRY was highly complex in its verse patterns as well as its imagery. In about 1220, Snorri Sturluson took it upon himself to compile a handbook for young poets wishing to learn the trade. This was the *Prose Edda*, a vital work for scholars today, for it deciphers the difficult codes of skaldic verse, which would otherwise be incomprehensible. In his *Edda*, too, Snorri explains the allusions to pagan gods and heroes found in the works of the old poets and so provides priceless insights into the myths and beliefs of the Vikings.

In pagan times, the Vikings believed that existence was governed by gods and goddesses, who belonged to two groups: the Aesir and the Vanir. The larger family was the Aesir, headed by Odin, the All-Father. War chief and god of the occult, he was a complex figure with sinister traits that called, in particular, for dark acts of sacrifice. Warriors slaughtered victims for Odin to ask him for victory, and then to thank him if he provided it. One custom was to dedicate the enemy's entire army to Odin – this involved the complete annihilation of the opposing forces, together with the destruction of all their belongings. In various bogs in Scandinavia the remnants of large sacrifices containing partially destroyed weapons have been found. One site in Gotland has yielded more than 500 spears, arrowheads and other articles.

The wild and unpredictable Odin was worshipped especially by warriors, chieftains and kings, and he carried a great

MASTER OF MAGIC   Image of a pagan
god, probably Odin, from Denmark.

has yielded the most sumptuous grave finds from the Viking Age. The occupants – a high-born woman and her female companion – were laid to rest in a chamber behind the ship's mast, with a marvellous array of accessories for the afterlife: a lavishly carved ceremonial wagon, sledges, beds, kitchen utensils, oil lamps, storage chests, tapestry and much more besides. Dating of the ship's timbers reveals that the burial dates back to 834. All had been wonderfully preserved by the mound of blue clay that had been heaped over the vessel.

High-ranking Vikings were often laid to rest in a boat, suggesting the belief that death involved a journey to reach the next world. Sometimes, instead of burying a chieftain in his ship, the Vikings would dress him in his finery and set the vessel alight with flaming torches. Where real boats were not used, people were often laid to rest in boat-shaped settings of stones for the symbolic voyage to the Beyond. One of the greatest Viking burial grounds is at Lindholm Høje in northern

### THE LONGER LIMB

Viking men had one arm longer than the other. Study of skeletons shows that their right arm was longer than the left. In women, arms were virtually equal. Presumably, men used their right arms more than their left for lifting heavy implements and weapons, while women used both arms equally.

Jutland where the ground is eerily patterned with a whole fleet of stone-outlined ships, one of them 75 ft (23 m) long.

In the municipal cemeteries of Viking towns there was less room for elaborate symbolism, and the dead were often laid to rest in simple pits, with or without a wooden coffin. At Birka in Sweden, 3000 graves have been identified. Cremation was clearly common practice, and the Vikings burned

**FEMALE BURIAL** A grave excavated at Birka revealed a woman laid to rest with her jewel box and household utensils.

the bodies clothed and adorned with jewellery. The charred bones and melted ornaments were then collected up for disposal, sometimes in a pot which was buried in the earth. Examination of Birka's cremated remains reveals that people were incinerated with a wealth of different items, from glass beads, knives, whetstones and gaming pieces to a dog, a sheep or occasionally a horse.

### THE ANGEL OF DEATH

Sometimes a high-ranking Viking took more than grave goods and animals into the Beyond. In a grave excavated at Stengade, Langeland, Denmark, archaeologists came upon the remains of two bodies, laid side by side with a spear placed obliquely across them both. One was of a master, the other of his slave. The thrall's feet were bound together and his head lay at an awkward angle; evidently he had been decapitated at the time of the funeral, and consigned to eternity with his master.

Several similar double burials have come to light, showing that the funeral sacrifice of slaves or consorts was by no means uncommon in Scandinavia. The macabre practice is reported also by

**GHOST SHIPS** Stones placed in boat-shaped patterns, set up to convey spirits into the afterlife, mark the ground at Lindholm Hoje in Denmark.

the Arab writers who observed the Vikings in Russia. The 10th-century traveller Ibn Rustah wrote: 'When a great man dies among the Rus, they make a grave like a large house and place him in it. His clothes, his arm-rings, some coins, large quantities of food and bowls of drink are put in with him. They also lay his favourite wife in the grave with him while she is still alive. Then, the mouth of the grave is blocked up and she dies there.'

Even more sensational is the account of the 10th-century Arab envoy, Ibn Fadlan, of the burial of a Rus chieftain on the Volga. In a long and extraordinarily vivid report he describes how the

**GRAVE TREASURE**
**A silver brooch found in the burial ground at Lindholm Hoje.**

Viking leader is laid in a temporary grave for ten days while his funeral costume is prepared. Meanwhile, his slave women are asked who wants to die with him. One of them volunteers and is thereafter tended constantly by two other women servants, who pamper her even to the extent of washing her

*continued on page 139*

# A Viking Ship Funeral

A HIGH-RANKING Viking was sometimes sent to eternity in his or her ship, which might be buried in the ground or set ablaze. The Arab, Ibn Fadlan, watched a boat burial in Russia where a chieftain was laid to rest with a sacrificed slave girl. Richly furnished with beautiful armour, carved chairs and beds, the death ship was drawn up on dry land and surrounded with firewood. At the appointed time, the dead chieftain's nearest kinsmen ignited the fire, and others followed, tossing on more burning brands. Sometimes a Viking might be buried in a boat-shaped setting of stones as a symbolic alternative to a wooden vessel. In these cases, too, the body was often disposed of by fire. At Lindholm Hoje in northern Jutland, for example, stones set in the outline of a ship surround cremations.

# HEALTH AND HYGIENE

THE SKELETONS recovered from Viking graves reveal much about the people's physical condition. Unlike their counterparts elsewhere in Dark-Age Europe, the Vikings were, on average, almost as tall as modern Europeans: the men about 5 ft 8 in (1.7 m); the women 5 ft 2 in (1.6 m). Bodies of over 6 ft (1.8 m) have also been found. The corpses recovered from the richer graves were markedly taller than those in the poorer, reflecting how much better the wealthier Vikings ate than did those who were poor.

Further investigation of the bodies revealed widespread evidence of osteoarthritis – a chronic inflammation of the joints, especially those that have to bear heavy weight. This must have resulted from heavy work in the fields and elsewhere. Lice and fleas clearly caused discomfort, and poor hygiene also contributed to stomach disorders. All bodies recovered from Viking York showed evidence of gutworms, whose eggs were found in cesspits and elsewhere. These intestinal parasites could grow to 1 ft (30 cm) inside the human gut, though they did not cause pain commensurate with their length. Investigators reckon that poisonous weeds such as corncockle, which turn up in the grain of Viking bread, probably caused more stomachaches than the gutworms ever did.

Viking medicine was primitive, though some attention was given to the treatment of battle wounds. One of the sagas describes how the women tended the casualties in a barn after a clash of arms, heating up water and dressing wounds. More impressively, a test meal was prepared for the purposes of diagnosis: the women made a porridge of onions and herbs, and when an injured man ate it the wound in his belly was examined. If the smell of onions and herbs issued from the wound it proved that the spear or sword thrust had penetrated his intestines and that he would likely die.

War casualties apart, the picture that emerges is of a healthy people by the standards of the day. Teeth, though worn down by coarse food, were in better overall condition than among present-day Scandinavians, because having no sugar the Vikings succumbed less easily to dental caries – cavities in the teeth.

Altogether, the evidence suggests that those Vikings who did not die in battle could expect a reasonably long life. In Denmark, where the most detailed studies have been done, examination of 240 adult skeletons demonstrated that the majority – 140 people – lived to the mature years of 35-55; 100 people lived to 20-35.

**SKELETAL REMAINS   A Viking burial in York. Evidence suggests that people were healthy by Dark-Age standards.**

feet. Throughout the waiting period 'the doomed woman drank and sang as though in anticipation of a joyous event'.

On the day of the funeral the chieftain's ship is brought ashore and dragged onto a huge heap of wood. A bier is placed on board and draped with Byzantine silks by an old woman called the Angel of Death, whose job it is to dress the chief's corpse and attend to the sacrifice of the slave girl. The dead man is now brought from his temporary grave and clothed in rich garments, gold-buttoned and trimmed with sable, which have been specially made for the occasion.

Propped up with cushions in a tent on board ship the corpse is furnished with alcoholic drink, bread, meat, onions, fruits and aromatic herbs. All his weapons are brought to him, and a dog, two horses, two cows, a cock and a hen are slaughtered and thrown into the ship. While these preparations are being made, Ibn Fadlan reports, the slave girl destined for sacrifice goes round to every tent in the camp and has sex with each owner, saying: 'Tell your master: I did this out of love for him.'

There follows an extraordinary rite in which the chief's followers raise the slave girl three times above a structure resembling a door frame. She cries out that she can see first her parents; then her dead relatives; and lastly her master sitting in a beautiful, green paradise with his men in attendance: 'He calls on me. Let me join him then!'

In the final act of this macabre drama the slave girl removes her jewellery, drinks down two beakers of *nabid*, or Nordic beer, and enters the tent where her dead master awaits. Again she has intercourse with men from the camp, and – as shields are beaten with sticks to drown her cries – a noose is placed round her neck. Two men pull the ends of the cord while the woman known as the Angel of Death stabs her to death.

Afterwards the chieftain's nearest kinsman lights the firewood under the ship. Then flaming

**ETERNAL SLEEP** Equipment for the afterlife might include weapons, food and utensils, and a human companion to serve the master in the Beyond.

**MEMORIALS** Burial mounds at Uppsala in Sweden. A grave might also be marked by a pole or by stones.

brands are tossed onto the pyre by the other people attending, and all is consigned to oblivion. Within an hour the pyre, the ship and its contents are reduced to a pile of ashes. The spot is then marked with a mound of earth, and a wooden post with the dead man's name carved on it is erected on the mound.

# THE COMING OF CHRIST

A barbaric warrior people who once murdered churchmen and plundered their monasteries

was conquered in the end by Christianity. Conversion came slowly in the Scandinavian homeland,

however – and Gospel preaching was not the only means by which it was brought about.

THE WILD GODS of the Norsemen were already something of an anomaly in Europe at the dawn of the Viking Age. Lying beyond the northern edge of Christendom, Scandinavia was a last bastion of paganism in a continent where priests and monks were increasingly acknowledged as the guardians of spiritual truth. Though Norse worship of the old gods did not end suddenly, Scandinavians were aware of Christianity throughout the Viking period, and those who went trading abroad must often have been awed by the great stone-built cathedrals and monasteries of Europe and Byzantium.

The early sea raiders may have seen church buildings only as treasure-houses ripe for plunder. But for the merchants and settlers who followed in their wake, the experience was different. They mixed with the local people, put down roots in Christian communities and in many cases became baptised Christians themselves. Conversion did not always involve a profound spiritual reorientation. A trader might, for example, accept the sign of the cross in order to do business with clients; a chieftain to seal a political alliance.

Many a Viking found it possible to worship Christ and the pagan gods simultaneously. The sagas report on an early settler of Iceland, called Helgi the Skinny, who was 'very mixed up in his faith; he believed in Christ, but prayed to Thor on sea journeys and in tough situations'. From Denmark, meanwhile, archaeologists have recovered a smith's mould that was used for making amulets in the form both of Thor's hammer and the Christian cross. There may have been some clients who bought both in order – like Helgi – to hedge their bets.

Conversion did not come only through chance encounters between Vikings and Christians. Frankish missionaries risked entering pagan Scandinavia as

MARK OF CHRIST  An axe blade with a cut-out cross possibly symbolises Christian faith and authority.

early as the beginning of the 8th century, when a certain Willibrord, the 'Apostle of the Frisians', made a failed attempt to convert the king of the Danes. Further efforts were made by the Frankish monk, Ansgar, who visited Jutland and central Sweden in the 9th century. Ansgar preached especially in the merchant centres of Hedeby and Birka frequented by Christian traders, and was able to found churches there. He even won permission for church bells to be rung at Hedeby, to the annoyance of pagan traditionalists. It was not piety, however, that encouraged the authorities to relent. They knew that Christian traders would be all the more likely to visit their town if they could attend church services there. Haarik the Elder and Haarik the Younger,

SMITH'S MOULD  A device for casting both Christian crosses and Thor's hammers.

## STAVE CHURCHES

**PLACE OF WORSHIP** Stave churches such as this one at Fagusnes, Norway, were probably modelled on earlier pagan temples.

As 11TH-CENTURY Scandinavia was brought within the fold of Christendom, a new type of religious building sprang up. This was the stave church, a basically rectangular construction walled with vertical timbers. These were held together by horizontal timbers at top and bottom, and the walls were raised slightly off the ground to prevent them from rotting. Stave churches were particularly common in Norway, and an exceptionally fine 12th-century example survives at Borgund, with dragonheads snarling out amid its clustered roofs.

A delightful little stave church at Urnes, not far away, includes some 11th-century decorated timbers carved with interlacing patterns made up of animals biting one another. The motifs demonstrate how close the Scandinavians still were at this time to their ancient, magical beliefs: a panel at Urnes depicts a stag nibbling at Yggdrasil, the World Tree of pagan mythology.

the Danish kings who permitted church-building, nevertheless held back from personal conversion, and it was in vain that the Pope himself made this urgent appeal: 'Stop worshipping false gods and serving the devil, for your gods are made with human hands and are deaf, dumb and blind. How can they save you when they cannot save themselves?'

Undaunted by setbacks and spates of pagan backlash, the missionaries extended their field of operations to Norway and Sweden. Ansgar was made archbishop of a new see at Hamburg-Bremen that became the centre for missionary activity in all Scandinavia, and converts were won in the very cradle of the Norse terror. The appeal of Christianity to the

Viking farmhand or housewife was the same as its appeal to common folk elsewhere in Europe: its paradise was open to the poor. While Odin's Valhalla was only for chosen warriors, any man or woman could earn a place in a heavenly hereafter by dint of a godly life. Many early missionaries earned respect for their piety and good deeds, through giving alms to the needy, and by redeeming slaves.

### POPPO'S MIRACLE

While piecemeal conversions broadened the base of Christianity in Scandinavia, the main strategy of the Roman Church was to try to win over the kings and chieftains. Both fair means and foul were

141

ROYAL CONVERSION  **A Danish altarpiece depicts the baptism of King Harald Bluetooth.**

employed in the quest for converts: it is said that in 934 a Danish king was forcibly baptised by German conquerors at Hedeby. For the Church, however, the real breakthrough came in about 960 when Denmark's King Harald Bluetooth converted voluntarily to the faith of Christ. It is reported that the king was won over by a bold little priest called Poppo who engaged the monarch in theological debate. The Danes admitted that Christ was a god,

### RUNIC GRAFFITI

The habit of scratching graffiti is not a modern phenomenon. A Viking called Halfdan carved his name in runic characters on a balcony of the great church of Hagi Sofia in Constantinople (Istanbul), where it survives to this day amid other names scrawled in later centuries by countless visitors.

but insisted that other gods were mightier, their signs and wonders more impressive. No, replied Poppo: the pagan gods were mere idols, and only the Holy Trinity was truly divine. King Harald, it is said, asked Poppo if he would put his beliefs to the test and there followed a miracle. Poppo 'picked up red hot iron bars and showed his unscorched hands to the King. Thereafter, King Harald and the whole Danish army were baptised.'

A large runic stone was carved at Jelling in Jutland to celebrate Harald's introduction of Christianity into Denmark. But it is likely that a shrewd sense of his own political interests motivated the king. Through conversion he would avoid unnecessary struggle with the German emperor to the south, and also help to consolidate his authority within his own kingdom.

*continued on page 145*

# MYSTERIOUS MONUMENTS AT JELLING

BROODING OVER the modern Danish town of Jelling are two gigantic ceremonial mounds from the Viking Age. And situated between the mounds is the oldest surviving church in Denmark. Here pagan and Christian monuments combine to make one of the finest and most enigmatic sites in Scandinavia.

Of the two great mounds, the one lying to the north is the largest of all Danish burial mounds. When in 1820 the local villagers dug their way in, they found a wooden chamber at the heart, subsequently dated to 958 or 959. The grave, however, was empty.

The South Mound, dated to about 960, is larger than the North Mound, but contains no burial chamber at all. Its purpose is uncertain; it may have been a memorial, or served as a platform for some now-forgotten ceremony.

How can the empty burial chamber be explained? Exactly half way between the two mounds King Harald Bluetooth raised a superb rune stone in memory of himself and his parents, with

SACRED SITE   The twin mounds at Jelling in Denmark, with the medieval stone church standing between them

an inscription commemorating the fact that he converted the Danes to Christianity. A relief of Christ's crucifixion is carved on one side of the massive stone, which was raised in about 985. Harald also had a large wooden church built just to the north of the stone, with an impressive grave in it. Investigation revealed that the grave contained the incomplete skeleton of a man who had evidently been moved to the spot after first being buried elsewhere.

Piecing together the clues, archaeologists have concluded that the body is that of Harald's father, King Gorm (who raised a rune stone of his own at the site). It is thought that Gorm was given a pagan burial in the North Mound, but when King Harald became a Christian he had his father's body transferred to the new church.

ROYAL RUNES   Christ is depicted on King Harald's great rune stone at Jelling. This is a modern replica, painted to show how it once looked.

## 800 – 849 AD

**COIN** A longship is depicted on a silver coin dated around 825, from Hedeby.

**800** Large quantities of Arab silver start to circulate in Scandinavia.

**808** The Danish king, Godfred, extends the Danevirke fortification as a defence against the Frankish emperor, Charlemagne.

**820s** Christian missionaries visit Scandinavia. Ebo, Archbishop of Reims, preaches in Denmark (823); subsequently, the Frankish missionary Ansgar, 'The Apostle of the North', visits Denmark and Sweden.

**825** The first Viking coinage is

**DECORATION** Carving from a wagon found at Useberg.

issued, at Hedeby in Denmark.

**834** A high-ranking noblewoman and her companion are laid to rest in the Oseberg ship burial in Norway.

---

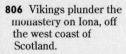

**806** Vikings plunder the monastery on Iona, off the west coast of Scotland.

**810** A large Viking fleet plunders Frisia, on the North Sea coast south-west of Denmark, forcing the inhabitants to pay 100 lb (45 kg) of silver in tribute.

**ROUND TOWER** A Celtic defence against Viking attack in Ireland.

**820** Viking ships loot the Aquitaine coast in southern France.

**830s** A decade of escalating raids sees renewed attacks by the Danes on England.

**834-7** The Vikings make annual assaults on the Frankish trade centre of Dorestad.

**839** Vikings set up their first winter camp in Ireland; settlement of Dublin follows in the 840s.

**841-4** Intensive raiding continues in France, with the sack of Rouen, Quentovic and Nantes. In 843 the Vikings start overwintering in Continental Europe.

**844** The first Viking expedition to Spain results in the conquest of Seville; Norse raiders withdraw, however, following a strong Moorish counterattack.

**845** Vikings sack Paris and Hamburg and reach far into Germany.

**846-7** The annual sacking of Dorestad resumes.

**SILVERWARE** Three 9th-century silver rings from Sandby in Sweden.

---

**800** Following conquests in northern Italy, Germany and Spain, Charlemagne is crowned Holy Roman Emperor by Pope Leo III. His empire, which includes most of western Europe, is almost as large as was that of the Romans.

The gigantic Buddhist shrine complex is built at Borobudur in central Java.

**810** Venice is recognised as an independent state by both Charlemagne and the Byzantine emperor. It flourishes as a trading centre, doing business with both empires.

**813** The Abbasid ruler, Mamun the Great, comes to power in Baghdad and establishes a 'House of Wisdom' there to foster learning.

**825** Irish monks are reported to be living in Iceland.

**843** By the Treaty of Verdun, Charlemagne's grandsons divide his

**CHARLEMAGNE** The Frankish emperor dominated 9th-century Europe.

empire between them, so diminishing imperial power.

**846** Rome is attacked by Arabs, who sack St Peter's and damage the Vatican.

**BUDDHIST SHRINE** A figure of the Enlightened One at Borobudur.

## 850 – 899 AD

### THE VIKINGS AT HOME

**GOKSTAD SHIP
The 9th-century vessel, seen at the Viking Ship Museum near Oslo.**

**850** The Gokstad ship burial at Vestfold, southern Norway, dates from around this time.

**850s** Ansgar revisits Denmark and builds churches at Hedeby and Ribe, where permission for bell-ringing is granted.

**860** Gorm the Elder unites the Danish islands with Jutland and becomes King of Denmark.

**880s** King Harald Finehair starts to unite Norway. Victory at Hafrsfiord near Stavanger (c.890) gives him control of the south and the coastal districts, but not the far north.

**890** The Svear people of central Sweden start to build the nucleus of a Swedish realm.

### THE VIKINGS ABROAD

**856-7** Vikings sack Paris, returning in 861 and 885-6.

**859-62** Norsemen raid in Spain and the Mediterranean.

**860** Vikings settle the Faeroe Islands.

**862** Swedish Vikings found Novgorod, the basis of the Russian state.

**865** A Viking Great Army lands in England, taking up winter quarters

**ENGLAND INVADED
A scene from a life of King Edmund.**

in East Anglia. It marches through England, seizing York (867), killing East Anglia's King Edmund (870), and doing battle with the Kingdom of Wessex (871).

**870** The Norse settlement of Iceland begins.

**873-4** The Vikings take up winter quarters at Repton, Derbyshire.

**878** Alfred the Great, King of Wessex, defeats the Vikings at Edington. The Treaty of Wedmore results in the partition of England: the Vikings keep their conquests in Mercia and East Anglia.

**THE DEFENDER
Statue of Alfred the Great at Winchester.**

### THE REST OF THE WORLD

**ALL SAINTS** The figures of St Gregory and St Cyril are represented above. Right: A mosaic image of St Basil.

**863** The Greek missionary St Cyril brings Christianity to the South Slavs of present-day Bulgaria and the Balkans. He is credited with inventing the Cyrillic alphabet.

**867** Basil I founds the powerful Macedonian dynasty in Byzantium, extending control over Asia Minor and southern Italy.

The Roman Catholic and Orthodox Churches divide.

**868** The first printed book, the Buddhist scripture *The Diamond Sutra*, is made in China.

**869** The island of Malta is captured by the Arabs.

**874** There is a popular uprising against the Tang Dynasty in China, which survives for another 30 years.

**875** The Magyar chieftain Arpad leads the Magyar tribe from the Caucasus into present-day Hungary and founds the first Hungarian royal dynasty.

**878** The island of Sicily is captured from the Byzantine Empire by the Arabs. They make Palermo the capital.

**879** Nepal gains its independence from Tibet.

**880** The city of Angkor is founded as capital of the Khmer Empire in Kampuchea.

**887** The final separation of France and Germany takes place following the dissolution of the Carolingian Empire.

**899** The Hungarians invade Germany.

# 900 – 949 AD

**SAXON KING** A 10th-century coin bears the image of Athelstan.

**930s** Archbishop Unni of the See of Hamburg-Bremen leads a Christian mission to the King of Denmark, Gorm the Old, father of Harald Bluetooth.

**930** Eirik I Bloodaxe, son of Harald Finehair, becomes King of Norway. He kills all his brothers and half-brothers (estimated to number about 40) but one, Hakon, who is reared as a Christian at the court of the English king, Athelstan.

**934** Eirik I is ousted from the throne of Norway because of the cruelty of his rule. He leads Viking expeditions to England, where he is granted charge of Northumbria by Athelstan and rules at York.

**935** Hakon the Good comes to the throne as Norway's first Christian king; he builds churches and brings priests from England.

**936** Harald Bluetooth becomes King of Denmark.

**948** In Denmark, bishops are appointed to Hedeby, Ribe and Arhus.

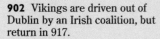

**VIKING HOARD** A 10th-century cache of silver from Lancashire.

**902** Vikings are driven out of Dublin by an Irish coalition, but return in 917.

**911** The Norse chieftain Rollo founds Normandy following victory at the Battle of Chartres. By 933, he and his successors have extended the territory to its present boundaries.

**912** Viking raiders attack Baku on the shores of the Caspian Sea.

**913** Edward the Elder drives the Vikings out of Essex.

**915** Unn the Deep-Minded settles in Iceland about this time.

**MEETING PLACE** Thingvellir, where Icelanders held the Althing, or national assembly.

**920** The English king, Edward, wins temporary control of Northumbria from the Vikings.

**922** The Arab envoy Ibn Fadlan meets Rus merchants on the River Volga.

**930** The Althing, or national assembly, is founded in Iceland to govern the country's affairs.

**937** The English under Athelstan win a famous victory over a coalition of Danes, Scots and Strathclyde Britons at 'Brunanburh' (a site not yet identified).

**900** The mysterious decline of the Mayan civilisation in Guatemala begins as people abandon their great ceremonial centres.

The Fujiwara family holds the monopoly of power in Japan.

**902** Work begins on the campanile of St Mark's Basilica, Venice.

**906** The Chinese Golden Age comes to an end with the final collapse of the Tang Dynasty; the country divides into many kingdoms.

**909** The Benedictine abbey of Cluny is founded by Duke William of Aquitaine. The first abbot is Berno of Baume, who instigates strict observance of the Benedictine Rule.

**929** St Wenceslas, King of Bohemia, is murdered by non-Christian rivals led by his younger brother, Boleslav I, when he submits to the German king to prevent an invasion of his country.

**930** Cordoba becomes the centre of Arab learning, science and commerce in Spain under the Caliph ruler Abd-al-Rahman III.

**938** The nomadic Khitan Mongols of northern China expand southwards and establish their capital at Beijing (Peking).

**939** Revolts against imperial rule in Japan spark off a period of civil war.

**945** Baghdad is captured by the Persians.

**MAYAN SITE** The Temple of the Masks at Tikal in Guatemala.

**TREASURES** Tang Dynasty relics display great artistry.

153

## THE VIKINGS AT HOME

**SWEDISH KING A coin bears the image of Olaf Skotkonung.**

**c.960** Harald Bluetooth, King of Denmark, converts to Christianity. He has a church built at Jelling where his father, King Gorm, is laid to rest after being removed from a pagan burial mound.

**964** Olaf Tryggvason becomes King Olaf I of Norway.

**968** Harald Bluetooth extends and refortifies the Danevirke to create a formidable barrier.

**987** Harald is exiled from Denmark, and is succeeded by Svein Forkbeard.

**995** Olaf I of Norway initiates the ruthless process of converting his people to Christianity, combined with attempts to unify his realm.

Olaf Skotkonung ascends the Swedish throne as the first king known to have ruled over both the Svear and the Gotar peoples of central and southern Sweden. Olaf

**DEFENCE WORK The Danevirke protected Denmark from attack.**

converts to Christianity, and mints Swedish coins at Sigtuna.

## THE VIKINGS ABROAD

**VIKING WEAPONS Axes and spears found in the River Thames.**

**954** Eirik Bloodaxe, the last Scandinavian king to rule at York, England, is ousted and dies in battle at Stainmore; the English king, Eadred, becomes ruler of all England.

**980** Viking rulers in Ireland are defeated at the Battle of Tara.

The Varangian Guard, made up of Viking warriors, is founded to provide a bodyguard for the Byzantine emperors.

**980s** A new wave of Viking attacks rocks England.

**985** Eirik the Red settles Greenland; Bjarni sights Vinland (in North America).

**c.990** Egil Skalla-Grimsson, hero of *Egil's Saga*, dies.

**991** The English are forced to pay Danegeld after defeat at the Battle of Maldon.

**994** Norway's Olaf Tryggvason unites with Denmark's Svein Forkbeard to mount a joint attack on London, again exacting tributes of Danegeld.

## THE REST OF THE WORLD

**955** Otto I, King of Saxony, defeats the Hungarians at the Battle of Lechfeld, outside Augsburg.

**960** The Song Dynasty is established in China and fosters commerce through the circulation of paper money, credit notes, and the manufacture of textiles, metalwork and porcelain.

**962** Otto I of Saxony is crowned Emperor by Pope John XII, and revives the Holy Roman Empire based on Germany and Italy.

**968** Cairo is founded by a leader of

**SILK MANUFACTURE Chinese textiles flourished under the Song Dynasty.**

the Fatimid sect, Jawhar, who invaded Egypt from Tunisia.

**969** The first playing cards, described as 'sheet dice', are reported in China.

**971** The eastern half of Bulgaria is conquered by the Byzantine Empire.

**977** Al Mansur becomes chief minister to the Omayyad Caliphate in Cordoba, Spain.

**980** Tula becomes the capital of the Toltec Empire in Mexico.

**983** Venice and Genoa develop a flourishing trade between western Europe and Asia.

**988** Byzantine civilisation spreads to Russia as Vladimir, Grand Prince of Kiev, converts to Christianity and

marries the sister of the Byzantine emperor. Within 50 years Kiev acquires 200 churches.

**992** Boleslav I begins the creation of the Polish state.

Otto III of the Holy Roman Empire makes Rome his imperial capital.

**994** Mahmud of Ghazni, Viceroy of Afghanistan, declares independence from the ruling Samanids of Bukhara.

**997** Stephen, a Christian and son of a Magyar chieftain in Hungary, defeats a pagan insurrection and the Hungarians convert to Christianity. Stephen is crowned King of Hungary.

**FLORAL VASE Song Dynasty porcelains are venerated by collectors.**

## 1000 – 1100 AD

**1000** Olaf Tryggvason, King of Norway, dies at the hands of the Danes in the Battle of Svolder.

**1015** Olaf II Haraldsson (later St Olaf) becomes King of Norway and uses terror to complete the conversion of his kingdom to Christianity.

**1019** Canute the Great, already Danish King of England, becomes King of Denmark.

MARTYRDOM  The death of King Olaf II, from a medieval manuscript.

**1028** Olaf II of Norway is overthrown by Canute the Great, who becomes King of Norway in addition to England and Denmark.

**1035** On the death of Canute the Great, his lands are divided between his sons: Hardecnut

becomes King of Denmark, Sweyn King of Norway, and Harold King of England.

**1047** A former Varangian guardsman, Harald Hardrada (Hard Ruler) becomes King of Norway.

**1066** Harald Hardrada dies at the Battle of Stamford Bridge, England. His death is often taken as the end of the Viking Age.

SILVER CROSS A Viking crucifix.

**1000** Iceland converts to Christianity.

Leif Eriksson, son of Eirik the Red, reaches Vinland from Greenland at about this time.

The Vikings are defeated at the Battle of Clontarf in Ireland.

**1016** Canute the Great becomes King of England and is the first Viking to rule the whole country. A Christian, he gives money to the Church and defends the country from attacks by other Vikings.

**1042** Death of Hardecnut, the last Viking king of England. He had succeeded his brother Harold.

**1066** The Norman conquest of England, led by William, Duke of Normandy, begins at the Battle of Hastings.

**1068** Birth of the Icelandic scholar, Ari the Learned.

CONQUERORS Details from the Bayeux tapestry show Norman ships sailing for Britain.

**1085** The Danes abandon a planned invasion of England.

FUNERARY MASK A product of Peru's pre-Inca Chimu people.

**1000** Precursors of the Inca culture begin to emerge in Peru, and kingdoms and cities start to appear.

**1031** The last Caliph of Cordoba loses his throne. Muslim Spain splits and many lands go to Christian kingdoms in the north.

**1042** The first use of movable type is recorded, in China.

**1044** The first known formula for gunpowder is published in China.

**1054** The split between the Eastern

Orthodox Church and the Church of Rome becomes permanent.

**1055** Seljuk Turks capture Baghdad. The Turks extend their rule over Persia, Iraq and (after 1071) Asia Minor.

**1059** Pope Nicholas II decrees that in future the Pope is to be elected by the cardinals, not by the clergy and people of Rome.

**1075** The Kingdom of Ghana is conquered by the Almoravids, Muslim warriors from the Sahara.

**1085** Alfonso IV of Castile captures Toledo from the Muslims. The Almoravids come to the aid of the Muslims but do not retake Toledo.

**1088** The first clock mechanism and the first magnetic compass are described in Chinese texts.

**1092** The Almoravids impose their rule on most of what remains of Muslim Spain.

SIEGE OF JERUSALEM  Crusaders capture the city in 1099.

**1094** El Cid, the Spanish national hero, takes Valencia from the Muslims.

**1096** The First Crusade is launched by Pope Urban II.

**1099** The Crusaders capture Jerusalem.

# INDEX

ACKNOWLEDGMENTS

ABBREVIATIONS T = Top; M = Middle; B = Bottom; R = Right; L = Left.

AAAC = Ancient Art and Architecture Collection, London.
BAL = Bridgeman Art Library, London.
ETA = E T Archive, London.
NHPA = Natural History Picture Archive.
TBA = Toucan Books Archive, London.
WFA = Werner Forman Archive, London.
YAT = York Archaeological Trust, York.

1 Warship prow/Weather vane, Knudsens/Giraudon. 2-3 The Gokstad Ship, AAAC. 4 Gosforth Cross: Thor Fishing for the World Serpent, C.M. Dixon, TL; Silver Armlet, Michael Holford, TR. 5 Manuscript Painting of Odin with Two Cows, Royal Library, Copenhagen/BAL, TL; Silver Cup, Lejre, Denmark, National Museum, Copenhagen, TR; Grave in the shape of a ship, Topham Picturepoint, BL; Ledberg Runestone, Sten-M. Rosenlund, BR. 6 Tombstone, Guildhall Museum, London, by Michael Holford. 7 Invasion of Danes under Hinguer (Ingvar) and Hubba, from *Life, Passions and Miracles of St. Edmund,* MS. 736, f.9v, Pierpont Morgan Library/Art Resource, New York. 9 Coppergate Dig, YAT, T; Glass Beads, WFA/Statens Historiska Museum, Stockholm, B. 10 Trelleborg Reconstruction, Lauros/Giraudon, T; Coin, WFA/British Museum, B. 11 Aerial View of Trelleborg, Comstock. 12-13 Norwegian Landscape, Robert Harding Picture Library; 13 Lava Field, Iceland, Zefa-Krecichwost, TR. 15 Cammin Casket, National Museum, Copenhagen, T; Turf Houses, Iceland, TRIP/H. Rogers, B. 17 Studded Casket from the Oseberg Ship Burial, University Museum of National Antiquities, Oslo, Norway, T; Bed from the Oseberg Ship Burial, University Museum of National Antiquities, Oslo, Norway, photographer: Kojan og Krogvold, B. 18 Rock-Carving at Ramsund, Södermanland, Sten-M. Rosenlund. 19 Cauldron, Knudsens/Giraudon, T; Flat Spoon, University of Trondheim, Vitenskapsmuseet, M; Round Spoon, YAT, B. 21 Grindstones, Rijksdienst voor het Oudheidkundig Bodemonderzoek, Holland, TL; Barley, NHPA/Rod Planck, TR; Viking Bread, ATA Stockholm, BR. 22 Soapstone Bowl, WFA/National Museum, Copenhagen. 23 Bayeux tapestry scene, Michael Holford, T; Drinking horn, AAAC, BL. 24 Cheese board, Foto Kulturen, Lund, Sweden - photograph: Lars Westrup, TL; Wooden bowls, YAT, TR; Glass cup, ATA Stockholm, B. 25 Manuscript illustration of Whaling, Stofnum Árna Magnússonar, Reykjavik, Iceland, T; Leister, University of Trondheim, Vitenskapsmuseet, B. 28 Oseberg tapestry, Knudsens/Giraudon, T; Harness-Bows, Mammen, National Museum, Copenhagen, B. 29 Lindholm Høje Field Strips, Aalborg Historiske Museum, TL; Wooden harrow, Viborg Stiftsmuseum/Guildager Fotografi, TR. 30 Frey, WFA/Statens Historiska Museum, Stockholm, TL; Freyja, WFA/National Museum, Copenhagen, TR; Bayeux tapestry scene, Michael Holford, B. 31 Bronze cow bell from Asheim Ostre, Seljord, Telemark, University Museum of National Antiquities, Oslo, Norway, T; Cattle stalls, Brattahlid, Eriksfjord, Greenland, R. Hall, B. 32 Danish coastline, Zefa-Schimnelpfennig. 33 Animal carving, YAT, T; Woodworking Tools, YAT, B. 34 Sandulf Stone, YAT. 36 Blacksmith's tools, SHM Bild, Stockholm, T; Detail of Stave Church carving: Regin the Smith, C.M Dixon, B. 37 Detail of tapestry, C.M Dixon. 38 Odindisa Runestone, Riksantikvarieämbetet/ Statens Historiska Museum, Stockholm/Bengt A. Lundberg. 39 Oseberg Cart: Mask Carving, WFA/Viking Ship Museum, Bygdoy. 42 Egil Skallagrímsson, Det Arnamagnæanske Institut, Copenhagen University. 43 Oseberg Cart: Carving, WFA/Viking ship Museum, Bygdoy, T; Pendant, WFA/Statens Historiska Museum, Stockholm, MR. 44 Stele, WFA, Statens Historiska Museum, Stockholm. 46 Gold Foils, WFA/Statens Historiska Museum, Stockholm. 47 Jewellery, Knudsens/Giraudon, TL; Brooch Pin, AAAC, TR; Arm Rings, AAAC, B. 48 Cloth Kit, YAT, T; Fabrics, YAT, B. 50 Leather Boots and Shoes, YAT. 51 Antler Combs, YAT. 53 Ball, Muzeum Naradowe, Szczecin, Poland, TL; Carved wooden boat, National Museum of Ireland, Dublin, TR. 54 Detail of wood portal carving: Sigurd kills Regin, WFA/University Museum of National Antiquities, Oslo, T; Silver Sword Hilt, Michael Holford, B. 55 Flateyjarbok, WFA/Stofnun Árna Magnússonar, Reykjavik. 56-57 Thingvellir, Mats Wibe Lund. 57 Lewis Chessmen: 'Beserk' Warrior, British Museum, London, TR. 58 Horsefight, WFA/Statens Historiska Museum, Stockholm, T; Bone Dice, YAT, B. 59 Nobleman hawking, Sockburn, YAT. 60 Hnefatafel Pieces, YAT, T; Boardgame Depicted on Runestone, Sten-M. Rosenlund, B. 61 Lewis Chessmen, C.M. Dixon, T; Flute, YAT, B. 62 Leather boot on skate, YAT. 63 Canterbury stained-glass roundel, Sonia Halliday Photographs. 64-65 Lindisfarne, Airfotos; 65 Lindisfarne Stone, YAT, TR. 66 Lindisfarne Priory, English Heritage Photographic Library, T; Oseberg Carving: Animal Head, Bridgeman/Giraudon, B. 67 Wood Carving, WFA/Maritime Museum, Bergen. 68-69 The Gokstad Ship, WFA/Viking Ship Museum, Bygdoy. 70 Bayeux tapestry scene, Michael Holford, BL. 71 Oar holes, YAT, T. 72 Oseberg Ship Sternpost, Knudsens/Giraudon. 73 Ship Graffito, National Museum of Ireland, Dublin. 72-73 Ship's anchor, WFA/Maritime Museum, Bergen. 74 Historical Excavation Photo of the Oseberg Ship Burial Mound, University Museum of National Antiquities, Oslo, Norway, T; Oseberg Cart, Robert Harding Picture Library, B. 75 Oseberg Carving: Symbolic Head, Knudsens/Giraudon, TR; Chariot with Four Wheels from the Oseberg Ship Burial, University Museum of National Antiquities, Oslo, Norway, B; 76 Oseberg Ship Burial: the Buddah Bucket, Knudsens/Giraudon. 77 Manuscript illumination of Arab Muslim soldiers from El Escorial Library, Madrid, Mas Photo Archive, ©Patrimonio Nacional, Madrid. 78 Warrior Cross Fragment, YAT, T; Shield Bosses, WFA/History Museum, Bergen University, B. 79 Mammen Axe, BAL/National Museum, Copenhagen, T; Helmeted Head of Warrior, AAAC, B. 80 Spear, WFA/National Museum of Copenhagen. 82 Pendant, WFA/Statens Historiska Museum, Stockholm, T; Kiev Helmet, YAT, B. 83 Manuscript, Topham Picturepoint/British Museum. 84 Danes Attacking a Town, from *Life, Passions and Miracles of St Edmund,* MS. 736, f.10, Pierpont Morgan Library/Art Resource, New York. 85 The Alfred Jewel, Ashmolean Museum, Oxford. 87 Kiev Suit of Armour, YAT. 88-89 Danevirke, National Museum of Copenhagen, T. 92-93 Iceland: Icebergs, NHPA/Patrick Foget. 93 Dried Lava Field, Images Colour Library, TL. 94 Manuscript: Grágás, Stofnun Árna Magnússonar, Reykjavik, TR. 96 Greenland, Zefa-Stockmarket. 97 Brattahlid, WFA, BL; Saga of Eirik the Red, AM. 554.4to, bl.f.96v, Det Arnamagnæanske Institut, Copenhagen University, Photo: Bent Mann, TR. 98 L'Anse aux Meadows Model, Parks Canada, Canadian Heritage, TL; Bronze Ringed-Pin, Parks Canada, Canadian Heritage, TR. 100 Flateyjarbok, Stofnun Árna Magnússonar, Reykjavik, T; Solar Compass, The National Museum, Copenhagen, Photo: Niels Elswing: MR. 101 Figure of Buddha, WFA/Statens Historiska Museum, Copenhagen,T; Gaming Pieces, WFA/Statens Historiska Museum, Stockholm, B. 104-5 1897 Photograph of Drawing of York in Caine's edition of the Analecta, British Library, T; Schist, YAT, BR. 106 Iron Artefacts, YAT. 108 Staraya Ladoga, Neil Price, T; Novgorad, St Sofia, Sigtuna Doors, Neil Price, B. 109 Sledge from the Oseberg Ship Burial, University Museum of National Antiquities, Oslo; photo: Ove Holst. 110 Russian Chronicle, AKG/Erich Lessing B. 111 Map of Constantinople, Sonia Halliday Photographs, T; Russian Chronicle, AKG/Erich Lessing, B. 112 Silver Hoard with Arab Coins, C.M. Dixon, T ; Weight, Roskilde Museum, Denmark, photo: Flemming G. Rasmussen, B. 113 Tapestry Detail, WFA/Statens Historiska Museum, Stockholm. 114 Furthark Inscription, Simon I Hill FRPS/'World of the Vikings' Sigtuna museer, YAT. 115 Standing Stones, Ale, Sten-M. Rosenlund. 116 Runestone: Alphabet, WFA/Statens Historiska Museum, Stockholm. 117 Rök Stone, Jan Rietz/Tiofoto; 118 Århus Runestone, Forhistorisk Museum, Moesgård; 119 Flateyjarbok, WFA/Stofnun Árna Magnússonar, Reykjavik. 120-1 Detail from the Frank's Casket, C.M. Dixon. 121 Codex Frisianus, AM. 45, bl.f.10v, Det Arnamagnæanske Institut, Copenhagen University, photo: Bent Mann, BR. 124 Detail of Stave Church Carving, Sigurd Tastes the Dragon's Blood, WFA/National Museum of Antiquities, Oslo; 125 Gotland Stone, WFA/Statens Historiska Museum, Stockholm, T; Pagan God, WFA/National Museum, Copenhagen, B. 126 Manuscript Ny Kgl Saml 1867.4 s.95v, BAL/Royal Library, Copenhagen, T; Bird Clasp, WFA/National Museum, Copenhagen, B. 127 Thor Hammer, WFA/Liverpool City Museum, Liverpool, T ; Manuscript: Thor, BAL/Royal Library, Copenhagen, B. 128 Loki, WFA /Århus Kunstmuseum. 129 Odin and Fenrir, WFA. 131 Flaxton Arm Ring, Photo: Simon I. Hill, Reproduced by courtesy of the Yorkshire Museum, YORYM 700.48, T; Hogback Tomb, WFA, B. 132 Stave Church, Urnes, WFA, T; Gold Arm-Ring, C.M. Dixon, B. 134-5 Lindholm Høje Burial Site, Comstock. 135 Silver Brooch, AAAC, TR. 138 Skeleton, YAT. 139 Uppsala Burial Mounds, Sten-M. Rosenlund. 140 Axe Head, National Museum, Copenhagen, T; Smith's Mould, WFA/National Museum, Copenhagen, B. 141 Stave Church, Fagusnes, WFA. 142 Harold Bluetooth's Baptism, C.M. Dixon. 143 Jelling Stone, TRIP/Photo: J. Braund/National Museum, Copenhagen, BL; Jelling Mounds, Nordam-Ullitz/Torkild Balslev, TR. 144 Gosforth Cross, Cumbria, C.M. Dixon. 145 Tapestry detail, WFA/Statens Historiska Museum, Stockholm. 146-7 Godafoss, C.M. Dixon. 147 Silver Crucifix, Birka, C.M Dixon. 148 Flateyjarbok, WFA/Stofnun Árna Magnússonar, Reykjavik, TL; Olavsantemensale, The Restoration Workshop of Nidaros Cathedral, Trondheim, TR. 149 Flatatunga Carving, WFA/Thjodminjasafn, Reykjavik, T; Bayeux tapestry detail, Michael Holford, B. 150 Sigurd's Helmet, WFA/Upplandsmuseet, Uppsala, TL; Animal's Head, C.M. Dixon, TR; Lindisfarne Priory, AAAC, ML; Lindisfarne Gospels, British Library, MR; Kiyomizu Temple, AAAC, BL; Chinese Miniature, Sonia Halliday Photographs, MB; Toltec Figures, Michael Holford, BR. 151 Hedeby coin, ATA, Stockholm/S.Hallgren, TL; Oseberg Wagon, Knudsens/Giraudon, TR; Celtic Tower, C.M. Dixon, ML; Permian Rings, Michael Holford, MR; Charlemagne, Sonia Halliday Photographs, BL; Borobodur, AAAC, BR. 152 Gokstad Ship, AAAC, TL; Manuscript MS. 736, f.7v, Pierpont Morgan Library/Art Resource, New York, ML; Alfred the Great, Sonia Halliday Photographs, MR; St Gregory and St Cyril, AAAC, BL; St Basil, AAAC, BR; Coin, AAAC, TL; Cuerdale Hoard, BAL/British Museum, TR; Thingvellir, Neil Price, ML; Mayan Temple, AAAC, BL; Tang Dynasty Art, AAAC, BMR; Camel, AAAC, BR. 154 Coin, Riksantikenvarieämbetet, Statens Historiska Museum, Stockholm, TL; Danevirke, Nordam-Ullitz/Torkild Balslev, TR; Axes, Museum of London, M; Chinese Engraving, Sonia Halliday Photographs, BL; Vase, AAAC, BR. 155 Saga of Saint Olaf, WFA/Stofnun Árna Magnússoner, Reyjkavik, TL; Pendant Crucifix, Michael Holford, TR; Bayeux tapestry details, Michael Holford, ML, MR; Peruvian Mask, AAAC, BL; Siege of Jerusalem, Michael Holford/British Library, BR.

Front cover: Det Arnamagnæanske Institut, Copenhagen University, T; British Museum, ML; Illustration by Paul Wright, MR; Michael Holford, MM; Illustration by Mel Wright, BL; National Museum, Copenhagen/ Werner Forman Archive, BR.

Back cover: Forhistorisk Museum, Moesgård, Denmark, T; Robert Harding Picture Library, TM; British Museum/Werner Forman Archive, ML; Lauros/Giraudon, MR; National Museum, Copenhagen, BL; Illustration by Mel Wright, BR.

The editors are grateful to the following individuals and publishers for their kind permission to quote passages from the books below:
The Bodley Head from *Vikings!* by Magnus Magnusson, 1980.
Everyman from *Egil's Saga* translated by Christine Fell, 1975.
Penguin Books Ltd from *The Vikings* by Johannes Bronstead, 1960; from *Vinland Sagas* translated by Magnus Magnusson and Hermann Palsson, 1965; from *Laxdaela Saga,* introduction and translation by Magnus Magnusson and Hermann Palsson, 1969; from *Hrafnkel's Saga and Other Stories* translated by Hermann Palsson, 1971; and from *The Vikings* by Else Roesdahl, 1991. Thames & Hudson Ltd from *The Vikings and their Origins* by David M. Wilson, 1989. Wayland (Publishers) Ltd from *The Vikings* by Michael Gibson, 1972.



59-012-1